THE
FOUR
INGREDIENT
COOKBOOK

By Linda Coffee and Emily Cale

Published by Coffee and Cale

The Four Ingredient Cookbook
Special Combination Edition

ISBN: 0-9677932-7-0

Published by:

cookbook resources
541 Doubletree Drive
Highland Village TX 75077
(972) 317-0245
Fax: (972) 317-6404
www.cookbookresources.com

Printed in the United States of America

For general information on Cookbook Resources books, including media kits, author appearances, discounts and premiums, contact: Sheryn Jones, (972)317-0245, email: sheryn@cookbookresources.com

For sales inquiries and special prices on bulk quantities of Four Ingredient Cookbook, contact Jerry Jones, (254) 791-8446 or
Email: jerry@cookbookresources.com

 I - 2

to our families

Meet the Authors

Emily Cale —

Born in San Antonio, Texas, Emily was raised in a military family who lived in Japan, Germany, Alaska and all over the United States. Now living in Kerrville, Texas, she is married with two children and two step-children, one graduated from college, two in college and one in high school (and the college students have all received copies of "The Four Ingredient Cookbook").

Emily has studied foreign gourmet cooking, and has participated in several gourmet cooking groups. Before moving to Kerrville, she worked at the United States Olympic Training Center in Colorado Springs. When she isn't busy promoting "The Four Ingredient Cookbook," she works at the Adult and Community Education Center for the Kerrville Independent School District.

Linda Coffee —

As a Home Economist, Linda worked in a foods and nutrition program as an Extension Agent for Texas A&M University. She has also been an interior designer and home designer, working with her husband's home building business.

The Coffees moved to Kerrville from Houston in 1977, in search of less traffic, a good environment to raise their two children, but the pace has been rather hectic! Their teenagers are active in football, track, volleyball and tennis.

Between her children's commitments, her husband's business and promoting "The Four Ingredient Cookbook," Linda finds time to teach a Special Education class at Tivy High School.

Seasonings

The seasoning or lack of seasoning in a recipe is often a matter of preference, a necessity of diet or a daring experiment. We encourage you to enhance any of these simple recipes by adding seasoning of your choice; therefore, we have often used the expression "season to taste."

Table of Contents

Appetizers

Cottage Cheese Dip

1) 1 (24 ounce) carton cottage cheese
2) 1 envelope Herb-Ox Dry Broth Mix
3) 1/3 cup milk
4) Chips or vegetables

Blend all ingredients, chill and serve with chips or fresh vegetables.

Dill Dip

1) 1 (12 ounce) carton cottage cheese
2) 2 1/2 teaspoons dill
3) 1/4 teaspoon seasoned salt
4) 2 tablespoons lemon juice

Combine all ingredients in blender. Blend at low speed. Refrigerate several hours for better flavor. Sprinkle with additional dill and serve with fresh vegetables.

Creamy Dill Dip

1) 1 cup Miracle Whip
2) 2 tablespoons onion, finely chopped
3) 1 tablespoon milk
4) 1 teaspoon dill

Mix all ingredients and chill. Serve with fresh vegetables.

Spring Vegetable Dip

1)   1 envelope dry vegetable soup mix
2)   1 pint sour cream
3)   Chips
4)   Vegetables

Combine soup mix and sour cream. Chill. Serve with chips or vegetables.

Sour Cream Dip

1)   1 cup sour cream
2)   1/2 tablespoon prepared mustard
3)   2 tablespoons chili sauce
4)   1/4 teaspoon celery seed

Combine all ingredients. Chill. Serve with celery sticks or cucumber slices.

Avocado and Leek Dip

1)   1 large ripe avocado, mashed
2)   1 tablespoon fresh lemon juice
3)   1/2 package dry leek soup mix
4)   1 cup sour cream

Mix mashed avocado with lemon juice. Combine with soup mix and sour cream. Serve with corn chips or tortilla chips.

Cream Cheese Dip

1) 1 (8 ounce) package cream cheese
2) 1 1/2 tablespoons lemon juice
3) 1 1/2 teaspoons onion, grated
4) 2 cups sour cream

Let cream cheese soften at room temperature. Cream until smooth. Add lemon juice and onion; blend well. Gradually blend in sour cream. Chill. Serve with potato chips, crackers or fresh vegetables.

Fresh Fruit Dip

1) Assorted fresh fruits, cut in bite-size pieces
2) 1 cup sour cream
3) 1 tablespoon brown sugar
4) Granulated sugar to taste (optional)

Mix sour cream and brown sugar. Add granulated sugar for desired sweetness. Serve with assorted fruits.

Sweet Fruit Dip

1) 1 (7 ounce) jar marshmallow cream
2) 1 (8 ounce) package cream cheese
3) 1 (8 ounce) carton sour cream
4) 1 (14 ounce) can sweetened condensed milk

Combine all ingredients in container of an electric blender and blend until smooth. Chill at least 1 hour. Serve with assorted fruits.

Tomato-Sour Cream Dip

1)   1 (8 ounce) can tomato sauce
2)   1 cup sour cream
3)   2 teaspoons grated onion
4)   1 teaspoon horseradish

Combine all ingredients. Chill. Serve with chips or fresh vegetables.

Hot Seafood Dip

1)   3 (8 ounce) packages cream cheese
2)   6 tablespoons milk
3)   2 tablespoons Worcestershire sauce
4)   1 (6 1/2 ounce) can crab meat

Soften cream cheese to room temperature. Mix all ingredients. Bake 15 minutes at 350 degrees. Serve with chips or crackers.

Chili Dip

1)   1 (15 ounce) can chili without beans
2)   1 (8 ounce) package cream cheese
3)   1/2 cup green chili sauce or jalapeno salsa
4)   1 (2 1/2 ounce) can sliced black olives, drained

Combine chili and cream cheese in pan. Cook over low heat until cheese melts, stirring occasionally. Stir in sauce and olives. Serve with tortilla chips.

Chili Con Queso I

1) 2 jalapeno peppers, reserve 1 tablespoon liquid
2) 1 (16 ounce) jar processed cheese spread
3) 1 (4 ounce) jar pimientos, drained and chopped
4) Chips

Seed jalapeno peppers and chop. Combine peppers, cheese spread and pimientos in saucepan. Heat on stove, stirring constantly, until cheese melts. Stir in reserved liquid. Serve with tortilla chips.

Chili Con Queso II

1) 1 pound Velveeta cheese, melted
2) 1 (15 ounce) can chili with beans
3) 1 (4 ounce) can green chiles, chopped
4) 1 medium onion, finely chopped

Mix all ingredients and bake in deep container for 35 minutes at 350 degrees. Serve with chips.

Zippy Cheese Dip

1) 1 pound ground beef
2) 1 pound Velveeta cheese, cubed
3) 1 (8 ounce) jar picante sauce
4) Chips

Brown ground beef and drain well. Melt cheese and add picante sauce. Combine meat and cheese mixture. Serve hot with tortilla chips.

Cheese Spread Dip

1) 1 (8 ounce) jar processed cheese spread
2) 2 tablespoons dry white wine
3) 2 teaspoons prepared mustard
4) 1/2 teaspoon Worcestershire sauce

Mix all ingredients. Chill. Serve with pretzels.

Hot Cheese Dip

1) 1 pound Velveeta cheese, cubed
2) 2 cups mayonnaise
3) 1 small onion, chopped
4) 3 jalapeno peppers, seeded and chopped

Place cheese in saucepan and melt over low heat. Add other ingredients and mix well. Serve with crackers or fresh vegetables.

San Antone Bean Dip

1) 1 (10 1/4 ounce) can condensed black bean soup
2) 1 (8 ounce) can tomato sauce
3) 1 cup sour cream
4) 1/2 teaspoon chili powder

Heat all ingredients in saucepan. Stir mixture occasionally. Serve with corn chips or tortilla chips.

Mexican Dip

1)   1 pound ground beef
2)   1/2 pound Mexican Velveeta cheese, cubed
3)   2/3 cup Miracle Whip
4)   1/4 cup onion, chopped

Season to taste and brown meat; drain. Add remaining ingredients and mix well. Spoon mixture on 9-inch pie plate. Bake 10 minutes at 350 degrees. Stir and continue to bake 5 minutes longer. Serve with corn chips.

Real Good Dip

1)   1 pound lean hamburger
2)   1 pound Jimmy Dean sausage (hot)
3)   1 pound Mexican Velveeta cheese, cubed
4)   1 can golden mushroom soup

Brown hamburger and sausage. Drain. Add cheese and soup and heat over low temperature until cheese is melted and thoroughly blended. Serve with tortilla chips.

Serving Idea: Form a "bowl" for serving dip by scooping out the center of a round, unsliced loaf of bread. Make croutons or bread crumbs from the bread when it has served its purpose as a "bowl".

Lobster Dip

1) 2 tablespoons margarine
2) 2 cups sharp American cheese, shredded
3) 1/3 cup dry white wine
4) 1 (5 ounce) can lobster, drained

Melt margarine and gradually stir in cheese. Break lobster into pieces. Stir in wine and lobster. Heat thoroughly and serve with chips or crackers.

Chili Ham Spread

1) 1 (4 1/4 ounce) can deviled ham
2) 1 tablespoon mayonnaise
3) 1 teaspoon grated onion
4   1 jalapeno pepper, finely chopped

Mix all ingredients. Spread on crackers.

Cottage Cheese-Cucumber Spread

1) 1 cup cucumber, finely chopped
2) 1 cup small curd cottage cheese
3) Dash pepper
4) Minced chives

Mix cucumber, cottage cheese and pepper. Spread on crackers and garnish with minced chives.

Hot Artichoke Canapes

1) 1 cup mayonnaise
2) 1 cup freshly grated parmesan cheese
3) 1 (4 ounce) can green chilies, chopped
4) 1 cup of canned artichoke hearts, chopped

Mix mayonnaise, parmesan cheese, green chiles and artichoke hearts. Put 1 teaspoon of the mixture on bite-size toast rounds. Broil until lightly brown.

Ricotta Crackers

1) Crackers (wheat, rye or any firm cracker)
2) 1 cup Ricotta cheese
3) 1/2 cup chutney
4) 1/4 cup nuts, chopped

Blend cheese and chutney and spread each cracker with mixture. Sprinkle with 1/4 teaspoon chopped nuts.

Hidden Valley Ranch Cheese Puffs

1) 2 cups shredded sharp cheddar cheese
2) 3/4 cup mayonnaise
3) 1 tablespoon Hidden Valley Ranch Milk Mix
4) 10 (1 inch) slices French bread

Mix first three ingredients. Spread on bread slices. Broil until golden brown (about 3 minutes).

Nutty Cream Cheese Spread

1)   2 (8 ounce) packages cream cheese
2)   1/2 cup sour cream
3)   1 (.4 ounce) package ranch style salad dressing
4)   1 (2 ounce) package pecan chips

Combine first 3 ingredients, stirring until blended. Chill 10 minutes. Shape mixture into a log. Lightly coat top and sides with pecans. Serve with crackers.

Pineapple Ball

1)   1 (8 ounce) package cream cheese
2)   1 (3 1/2 ounce) can crushed pineapple, drained
3)   2 tablespoons green pepper, chopped
4)   1 teaspoon Lawry's Seasoned Salt

Mix cream cheese, pineapple, green pepper and sprinkle with Lawry's Seasoned Salt. Shape into a ball and serve with crackers.

Shrimp Spread

1)   2 (4 1/2 ounce) cans shrimp, drained
2)   2 cups mayonnaise
3)   6 green onions, chopped fine
4)   Crackers

Crumble shrimp. Mix above ingredients and refrigerate for at least one hour. Serve with crackers.

Hot Celery Appetizer

1) Crackers or rye bread
2) 3 ounces cream cheese
3) 1/4 cup celery soup
4) 1 cup ground salami

Combine cream cheese, soup and ground salami. Spread mixture on crackers or bread. Heat under broiler until brown.

Deviled Ham Appetizer

1) Crackers
2) 1 (4 1/4 ounce) can deviled ham
3) 1/2 teaspoon lemon juice
4) 1/2 teaspoon Worcestershire sauce

Mix deviled ham, lemon juice and Worcestershire sauce. Spread on crackers.

Pizza Crackers

1) 4 dozen Melba or cracker rounds
2) 3/4 cup catsup
3) 2 ounces pepperoni, thinly sliced
4) 1 cup shredded mozzarella cheese

Spread rounds with catsup and top with pepperoni slices. Sprinkle with cheese and bake on cookie sheet 3 to 5 minutes at 400 degrees.

Easy Crab Spread

1) 1 (8 ounce) package cream cheese
2) 1 (12 ounce) bottle cocktail sauce
3) 1 (6 ounce) can crab meat, drained
4) Crackers

Spread cream cheese on dinner plate and pour bottle of cocktail sauce over cream cheese. Crumble crab meat on top of the cocktail sauce. Serve with crackers.

Garlic Loaf

1) 1 can refrigerated biscuits, separated
2) 1/2 cup margarine, melted
3) 1 teaspoon garlic powder
4) 1 tablespoon parsley

Cut each biscuit in half. Mix garlic, parsley and margarine. Dip biscuits in mixture and place in 9-inch pie plate. Bake 15 minutes at 400 degrees.

Crispy Cheese Bread

1) 2/3 cups crushed Rice Chex cereal
2) 3 tablespoons parmesan cheese
3) 2 tablespoons margarine, melted
4) 1 can refrigerated biscuits, separated

Combine cereal, cheese and margarine. Halve biscuits. Coat with crumb mixture. Place in 9-inch pie plate and bake 15 minutes at 400 degrees.

Sausage-Cheese Turnovers

1) 10 (1 ounce) link sausages, cooked until brown
2) 2 ounces sharp cheddar cheese strips
3) 1 (11 ounce) can refrigerated biscuits
4) 2 tablespoons cornmeal

Roll each biscuit into a 4-inch diameter circle; sprinkle with cornmeal. Center cheese strips and sausages on biscuits. Fold over and seal edges with fork dipped in flour. Bake 10 minutes at 400 degrees.

Bacon Roll-ups

1) 1/2 cup sour cream
2) 1/2 teaspoon onion salt
3) 1/2 pound bacon, cooked and crumbled
4) 1 (8 ounce) package crescent rolls, separated

Mix the top 3 ingredients; spread on rolls and roll up. Place on baking sheet. Bake 12 to 15 minutes at 375 degrees.

Morning Coffee Appetizer

1) 1 package pre-cooked pork link sausage
2) 1 package refrigerated butterflake rolls

Cut each sausage in thirds. Peel two thin sections off a butterflake roll; wrap around a small piece of sausage. Bake on ungreased cookie sheet 7 to 8 minutes at 450 degrees.

Sausage Cheese Balls

1) 1 pound hot pork sausage
2) 1 pound sharp cheddar cheese, grated
3) 3 cup biscuit mix
4) 1/4 to 1/2 cup water

Mix all ingredients and form into bite-size balls. Bake 10 to 15 minutes at 375 degrees.

Olive Cheese Balls

1) 2 cups shredded sharp cheddar cheese
2) 1 1/4 cups all-purpose flour
3) 1/2 cup margarine, melted
4) 36 small pimiento stuffed olives, drained

Mix cheese and flour; mix in margarine. From this dough mixture, mold 1 teaspoonful around each olive. Shape into a ball. Place on ungreased cookie sheet and refrigerate at least 1 hour. Bake 15 to 20 minutes at 400 degrees.

Party Biscuits

1) 1 cup self-rising flour
2) 1 cup whipping cream (not whipped)
3) 3 tablespoons sugar
4) Margarine to grease muffin cups

Mix ingredients and pour into greased mini-muffin cups. Bake 10 minutes at 400 degrees.

Cheese Rounds

1) 1 cup grated cheddar cheese
2) 1/2 cup margarine
3) 1 1/4 cups flour
4) Dash cayenne pepper

Mix ingredients and form long rolls 1-inch in diameter. When ready to bake, slice into 1/4-inch rounds and bake 5 minutes at 400 degrees.

Cheese Sticks

1) 1 loaf regular slice bread, crust removed
2) 1/2 cup margarine, melted
3) 1 cup parmesan cheese
4) 1 teaspoon paprika

Slice bread into thin sticks. Roll in melted margarine, then in parmesan and paprika. Place on cookie sheet. Bake 20 minutes at 325 degrees.

Beer Biscuits

1) 3 cups biscuit mix
2) 1/4 teaspoon salt
3) 1 teaspoon sugar
4) 1 1/2 cups beer

Mix all ingredients and spoon into 12 greased muffin cups. Bake 15 minutes at 425 degrees.

Party Rye Bread

1) 1 package party rye bread
2) 1 cup mayonnaise
3) 3/4 cup parmesan cheese
4) 1 onion, grated

Mix mayonnaise, cheese and onion. Spread on bread and broil 2 to 3 minutes.

Water Chestnuts

1) 2 (8 ounce) cans whole water chestnuts
2) 6 to 8 slices bacon, cut into quarters

Wrap each water chestnut with quartered strip of bacon. Secure with toothpick. Broil until bacon is cooked.

Water Chestnut Appetizers

1) 1 (8 ounce) can water chestnuts
2) 6 thin slices bacon, halved
3) 6 chicken livers, halved
4) Hot English mustard

Divide water chestnuts into 12 portions. Wrap each chestnut with liver, then a piece of bacon. Secure with toothpick and broil until bacon is crisp. Serve with hot English mustard as a dip.

Bacon Surprise

1) 1 pound bacon
2) 1/2 cup brown sugar
3) 1 (7 3/4 ounce) jar pickled onions, drained
4) Dash of dry mustard (optional)

Cut bacon into fourths. Wrap a piece of bacon around a pickled onion. Secure with toothpick and roll in brown sugar with an added dash of dry mustard (optional). Place on broiler pan and broil until bacon is crisp.

Fried Mozzarella

1) 8 ounces mozzarella cheese, cut in 1/2-inch cubes
2) 2 eggs, slightly beaten
3) 1 cup fine cracker crumbs
4) 2 tablespoons olive oil

Dip the cheese cubes into the egg and then into the cracker crumbs. Heat the oil in a skillet and fry the breaded cheese until crisp and brown. Stick each cube with a toothpick.

Vienna Cocktail Sausages

1) 2/3 cup prepared mustard
2) 1 cup currant jelly
3) 4 (4 ounce) cans Vienna sausages, halved
4) Pinch of salt (optional)

Mix mustard and jelly with a pinch of salt (optional). Add sausages; heat thoroughly; serve hot.

Jalapeno Pie

1) 1 (11 ounce) can jalapeno peppers
2) 3 eggs, beaten
3) 2 cups grated cheddar cheese
4) Salt and pepper, to taste

Seed and chop peppers. Place peppers in greased 9-inch pie plate. Sprinkle cheese over peppers. Pour seasoned eggs over cheese. Bake 20 minutes at 400 degrees. Cut into small slices and serve.

Deviled Eggs

1) 6 hard cooked eggs
2) 1 1/2 tablespoons sweet pickle relish
3) 3 tablespoons mayonnaise
4) Paprika

Peel eggs and cut in half lengthwise. Take yolks out and mash with fork. Add relish and mayonnaise to yolks. Place this yolk mixture back into the egg white halves. Sprinkle with paprika.

Preparation Idea: When grating cheese, brush the grater with oil or spray with no stick cooking spray for easy clean up.

Stuffed Mushrooms

1) 1 pound (half dollar size) mushrooms
2) 1 cup bread crumbs
3) 2 tablespoons margarine
4) 2 slices ham lunch meat, chopped

Remove stems and inside of mushrooms. Chop stems and mix with remaining ingredients. Stuff mushrooms and place in buttered casserole dish. Bake 15 minutes at 350 degrees.

Dried Beef Appetizers

1) 3 ounces cream cheese
2) 1/2 teaspoon minced onion
3) 3 ounces dried beef
4) 1/4 teaspoon garlic powder (optional)

Chop beef and add onion, cream cheese and garlic powder (optional). Form into small balls and refrigerate. Serve with toothpicks.

Serving Idea: Appetizers served individually on toothpicks can be stuck into a grapefruit for an easy, attractive way to serve.

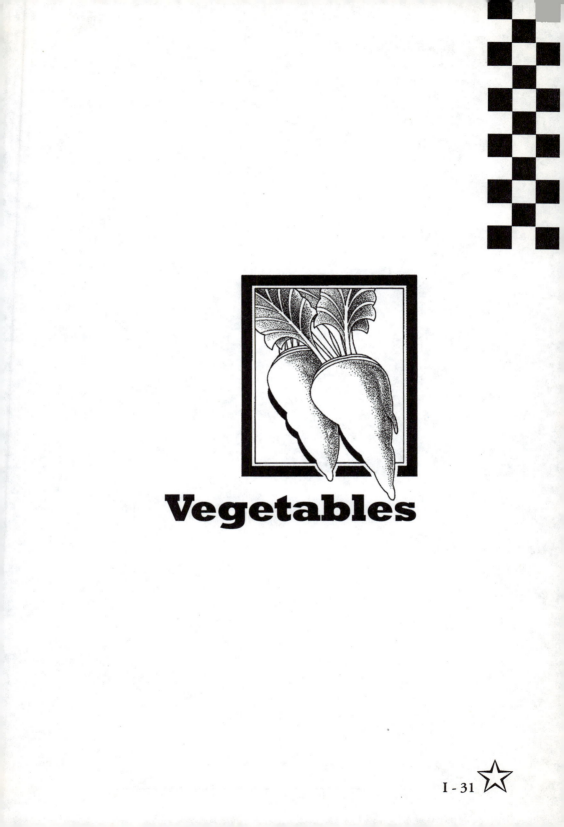

Vegetables

Asparagus Roll-Up

1) 4 slices ham
2) 4 slices Swiss cheese
3) 2 (10 1/2 ounce) cans asparagus spears
4) 1 cup sour cream

Place a slice of cheese on top of each ham slice. Put 3 asparagus spears on each ham/cheese slice. Roll up, secure with toothpick. Place in casserole, seam side down and spoon sour cream over each roll. Bake 15 minutes at 350 degrees. Serves 4.

Baked Beans

1) 2 tablespoons brown sugar
2) 1 tablespoon mustard
3) 1 cup catsup
4) 2 (15 ounce) cans pork and beans

Combine all ingredients. Bake 1 hour at 350 degrees. Serves 6 to 8.

Spicy Green Beans

1) 2 (16 ounce) cans green beans, drained
2) 4 slices bacon, chopped
3) 1 medium onion, chopped
4) 1/4 cup vinegar

Saute bacon and onion in skillet. Drain. Add green beans and vinegar and heat thoroughly.

Bush's Broccoli Salad

1) 3 cups broccoli, cut into bite-size pieces
2) 1 red onion, chopped
3) 1 cup cheddar cheese, grated
4) 6 slices bacon, cooked and crumbled

Combine all ingredients. Best when used with the following dressing. Serves 6 to 8.

Broccoli Dressing

1) 1 cup mayonnaise
2) 1/4 cup sugar
3) 2 tablespoons vinegar
4) Broccoli salad

Mix well and pour over broccoli salad.

Marinated Brussels Sprouts

1) 2 (10 ounce) packages brussels sprouts, cooked
2) 1/2 cup salad oil
3) 1/4 cup white wine vinegar
4) 1 package Italian salad dressing mix

Mix all ingredients and marinate overnight. Serve cold. Serves 6 to 8.

Hot Cabbage

1) 3 cups finely chopped cabbage
2) 1/2 teaspoon salt
3) 2 tablespoons vegetable oil
4) 2 tablespoons Italian salad dressing

Sprinkle cabbage with salt and set aside for 30 minutes. Heat oil in skillet until very hot. Add the cabbage and stir fry about 2 minutes. Remove and add Italian dressing. Serves 4.

Peachy Carrots

1) 1 pound package carrots, sliced and cooked
2) 1/3 cup peach preserves
3) 1 tablespoon margarine, melted
4) Pinch salt (optional)

Combine carrots with margarine and peach preserves. Add a pinch of salt (optional). Cook over low heat until carrots are heated thoroughly. Serves 6.

Carrot Casserole

1) 1 pound package carrots, sliced and cooked tender
2) 1/2 cup celery, chopped
3) 1/3 cup onion, chopped
4) 1/3 cup green pepper, chopped

Saute chopped celery, onion and green pepper. Mash cooked carrots and mix with sauteed vegetables. Put in buttered baking dish. Bake 30 minutes at 350 degrees. Serves 6.

Honey Carrots

1) 1 pound package carrots, peeled and sliced
2) 1/4 cup honey
3) 1/4 cup margarine, melted
4) 1/4 cup brown sugar, firmly packed

Cook carrots in small amount of boiling water for 5 to 10 minutes or until crisp-tender. Drain, reserve 1/4 cup of the carrot liquid. Combine reserved liquid, honey, margarine and brown sugar. Stir well and pour over carrots. Cook over low heat until heated thoroughly. Serves 6.

Cream Cheese Corn

1) 2 (16 ounce) cans whole corn, drained
2) 1 (8 ounce) package cream cheese
3) 1 (4 ounce) can green chiles, chopped
4) 1 tablespoon margarine

Combine ingredients in saucepan. Simmer over low heat until cheese melts. Mix well. Serves 4 to 6.

Corn Pudding

1) 2 (16 ounce) cans creamed corn
2) 1 (6 ounce) package corn muffin mix
3) 2 eggs, beaten
4) 1/2 cup margarine, melted

Mix all ingredients and pour into a greased 2-quart casserole dish. Bake 45 minutes at 350 degrees. Serves 6.

Corn Casserole

1) 2 (16 ounce) cans cream corn
2) 1/2 cup milk
3) 1 cup bread crumbs
4) 1/2 cup chopped green pepper

Mix all ingredients and pour into casserole. Bake 30 minutes at 350 degrees. Serves 4 to 6.

Okra Gumbo

1) 2 slices bacon, chopped
2) 1/2 cup onion, chopped
3) 1 (10 ounce) package frozen okra, sliced
4) 1 (14 1/2 ounce) can stewed tomatoes, chopped

Saute bacon, add onion and brown. Add frozen okra and stewed tomatoes. Cook over low heat until okra is tender. Season to taste. Serves 4 to 6.

Onion Custard

1) 4 to 6 medium mild onions, thinly sliced
2) 3 tablespoons unsalted butter
3) 1 cup milk
4) 3 eggs

Saute onions in butter in covered skillet for 30 minutes. Cool. In bowl beat together milk and eggs. Stir in onions and transfer to greased baking dish. Bake 40 to 50 minutes at 325 degrees or until light golden. Serves 6 to 8.

Baked Onion Rings

1) 2 egg whites
2) 1 large sweet yellow onion, cut into rings
3) 1/3 cup dry bread crumbs
4) Salt and pepper, to taste

Mix egg whites, salt and pepper. Dip onion rings into egg mixture and then coat with bread crumbs. Place in single layer on greased baking sheet. Bake 10 minutes at 450 degrees. Serves 4.

Souffle Potato

1) 2 2/3 cups mashed potato mix
2) 1 egg, beaten
3) 1 (2.8 ounce) can French fried onion rings
4) 1/2 cup shredded cheddar cheese

Prepare mashed potato mix according to package directions. Add egg, onions and stir until blended. Spoon mixture into a lightly greased 1-quart dish. Sprinkle with cheese. Bake uncovered 5 minutes at 350 degrees. Serves 6.

Baked Potato Topping

1) 1 cup grated sharp processed cheese
2) 1/2 cup sour cream
3) 1/4 cup soft margarine
4) 4 tablespoons chopped green onion

Mix all ingredients and serve on baked potato. Serves 4 to 6.

Twice Baked Potatoes

1) 4 baked potatoes
2) 4 tablespoons margarine
3) 1/2 cup milk
4) 1 cup grated cheddar cheese

Bake potatoes. Cut cooked potatoes in half. Scoop out meat of the potato and whip with margarine and milk. Mound back into the potato halves. Sprinkle with grated cheese. Bake 30 minutes at 350 degrees. Serves 4 to 8.

Sheepherder Potatoes

1) 8 bacon slices, minced
2) 2 onions, chopped
3) 4 potatoes, peeled, sliced 1/2 inch thick
4) Salt and pepper

Fry bacon until not quite crisp. Add onion and saute until limp. Pour off all but 2 tablespoons of drippings. Center potatoes on tin foil placed in large casserole dish. Pour bacon mixture over potatoes and season with salt and pepper. Seal foil with small space between potatoes and foil. Bake 1 1/2 hours at 300 degrees. Serves 4 to 6.

Preparation Idea: Freeze stale bread and then grate the frozen bread to use as vegetable or casserole toppers as needed.

Rice-Green Chili Casserole

1) 1 (4 ounce) can chopped green chilies, drained
2) 2 cups sour cream
3) 3 cups cooked white rice
4) 8 ounces Monterey Jack Cheese, grated

Combine chiles and sour cream. Place 1 cup cooked rice in bottom of 1 1/2 quart casserole. Spoon a third of sour cream mixture over rice and top with one third of the cheese. Do this two more times. Cover and bake 20 minutes at 350 degrees. Uncover and bake 10 minutes longer. Serves 6.

Mexican Rice

1) 1 cup uncooked Minute Rice
2) 1 green pepper, chopped
3) 1/2 medium onion, chopped
4) 1 (28 ounce) can tomatoes

Fry 3 tablespoons of the uncooked rice until brown. Add onions and green pepper and saute. Add rest of uncooked rice and can of tomatoes (add a little water if needed). Cover and simmer 1/2 hour. Serves 4 to 6.

Serving Idea: Many cooked vegetables taste wonderful just tossed with margarine. Add variety to the margarine with spices. For example, add 1 teaspoon celery seed or 2 tablespoons grated parmesan cheese or 1/4 teaspoon garlic powder to 1/4 cup margarine.

Snow Peas and Mushrooms

1)   1 cup sliced mushrooms
2)   2 tablespoons margarine
3)   1/2 pound small snow peas
4)   1 tablespoon soy sauce

Saute mushrooms in margarine. Stir in snow peas and soy sauce. Cook until crisp-tender. Toss and serve. Serves 4.

Squash Casserole

1)   6 medium yellow squash, sliced
2)   1 small onion, chopped
3)   1 cup Velveeta cheese, cut in 1/2 inch cubes
4)   1 (4 ounce) can chopped green chilies

Boil squash and onion until tender. Drain well and mix with cheese and chiles. Pour into buttered baking dish. Bake 15 minutes at 375 degrees. Serves 6 to 8.

"Hot" Zucchini Squash

1)   5 to 6 medium zucchini, sliced in round
2)   1 cup grated Monterey Jack jalapeno cheese
3)   1/2 cup bread crumbs
4)   1 (14 1/2 ounce) can stewed tomatoes, chopped

Boil zucchini for 8 minutes until crisp-tender. Place 1/2 of zucchini in greased casserole and sprinkle with cheese and crumbs. Top with remainder of zucchini. Cover with tomatoes. Bake 30 minutes at 350 degrees. Serves 6 to 8.

Zucchini Squash Fritters

1) 2 medium zucchini, grated
2) 1 carrot, grated
3) 1 egg, beaten
4) 1/2 cup flour

Mix all ingredients. Drop by tablespoon into 1/2-inch oil in skillet. Fry until golden brown. Drain on paper towel and serve. Serves 4 to 6.

Spinach Casserole I

1) 1 (16 ounce) carton cottage cheese
2) 8 ounces sharp cheddar cheese, grated
3) 1 (10 ounce) package chopped spinach, drained
4) 3 eggs, beaten

Combine all ingredients and mix well. Spoon into buttered casserole. Bake 45 minutes at 350 degrees. Serves 6.

Spinach Casserole II

1) 3 (10 ounce) boxes frozen chopped spinach
2) 1 cup sour cream
3) 1 envelope dry onion soup mix
4) Sprinkle bread or cracker crumbs (optional)

Thaw spinach, press out water. Mix with sour cream and dry onion soup mix. Sprinkle with bread or cracker crumbs if desired. Bake 20 to 25 minutes at 325 degrees. Serves 8 to 10.

Sweet Potato and Apple Bake

1)   6 large sweet potatoes, peeled, sliced, boiled
2)   6 tart apples, peeled and sliced
3)   1/2 cup margarine
4)   1/2 cup brown sugar

Grease casserole with part of margarine. Layer potatoes, dot with margarine and sprinkle with brown sugar, layer with apple slices. Repeat, ending with potatoes, margarine and brown sugar. Bake 30 to 45 minutes at 350 degrees, or until potatoes are tender and browned. Serves 8 to 10.

Tomato Stack

1)   1 (10 ounce) package frozen chopped broccoli
2)   1 cup grated Monterey Jack cheese
3)   1/4 cup finely chopped onion
4)   3 large tomatoes, halved

Cook broccoli as directed. Drain and mix with cheese, reserve 2 tablespoons of cheese for top. Add onion. Place tomato halves in greased baking dish. Place broccoli mixture on each tomato half and top with reserved cheese. Broil 10 to 12 minutes at 350 degrees. Serves 6.

Cold Vegetable Dish

1)   1 basket cherry tomatoes
2)   1 bunch broccoli, fresh and cut up
3)   1 head cauliflower, fresh and cut up
4)   1 (8 ounce) bottle Italian salad dressing

Mix above ingredients the day before you are ready to serve. Serve cold. Serves 8 to 10.

Main Dishes

Beef-Rice Casserole

Bake 350 Degrees   1 Hour

1) 1 pound ground round or lean chuck
2) 2 cans cream of onion soup
3) 1 package dry onion soup mix
4) 1 cup rice, uncooked

Mix all ingredients. Put in baking dish and bake covered.
Serves 4 to 6.

Poor Man Steak

Bake 325 Degrees   1 Hour

1) 3 pounds ground beef
2) 1 cup cracker crumbs
3) 1 cup water
4) 1 can cream of mushroom soup

Combine ground beef, cracker crumbs, water and season to taste.
Form into serving size patties and brown in skillet. Remove
browned beef and put in oven roaster. Spread soup on top and
bake covered. Serves 8 to 10.

Indian Corn

Stove Top

1) 1 pound lean hamburger
2) 1 (16 ounce) can whole corn, drained
3) 1/2 onion, chopped
4) 1 (12 ounce) jar taco sauce

Brown hamburger and onion; add corn and taco sauce. Simmer
mixture for 5 minutes. Serve with tortilla chips. Serves 4 to 6.

BBQ Cups

Bake 400 Degrees   12 Minutes

1) 1 pound lean ground beef
2) 1/2 cup barbeque sauce
3) 1 can refrigerator biscuits
4) 3/4 cup grated cheddar cheese

Brown meat, drain. Add barbeque sauce and set aside. Place biscuits in ungreased muffin cups, pressing dough up sides of edge of cup. Spoon meat mixture into cups. Sprinkle with cheese. Bake. Serves 4 to 5.

Hamburger in Oven

Bake 350 Degrees   30 Minutes

1) 2 pounds extra lean ground beef
2) 2 medium onions, sliced thin
3) 1 (32 ounce) package frozen French fries
4) Salt and pepper

Divide meat into 6 to 8 equal parts and make into patties. Season to taste. Place on foil in large baking pan and arrange onion slices on top of each patty. Place fries around them. Wrap foil tightly and bake. Serves 6 to 8.

Tater Tot Casserole

Bake 350 Degrees   1 Hour

1)   2 pounds extra lean ground beef
2)   1 can cream of mushroom soup
3)   1 cup grated cheddar cheese
4)   1 (2 pound) package frozen tater tots

Pat ground beef in bottom of greased 13x9x2-inch pan. Spread soup over meat and cover with grated cheese. Top with tater tots. Bake covered 45 minutes and uncovered 15 minutes. Serves 8 to 10.

Salisbury Steak

Stove Top

1)   1 pound lean ground beef
2)   1 egg
3)   1 medium onion, chopped
4)   1 beef bouillon cube, dissolved in 1/2 cup water

Mix beef, egg and onion. Shape into patties and brown over high heat, drain off any fat. Pour in bouillon and simmer uncovered until desired doneness. Serves 4.

Beef Patties

Stove Top

1)   1 pound ground beef chuck
2)   1 cup mashed potatoes
3)   2 tablespoons onion, minced
4)   2 tablespoons margarine

Mix beef, potatoes, onion and form into patties. Brown slowly in margarine until desired doneness. Serves 4 to 6.

"Fast" Food Mexican

Bake 350 Degrees   30 Minutes

1) 1 dozen tamales, wrappers removed
2) 1 (15 ounce) can chili
3) 1 cup chopped onions
4) 1 1/2 cups grated cheddar cheese

Place tamales in greased casserole, top with chili and sprinkle with cheese and onions. Bake. Serves 4.

Quick Enchiladas

Bake 350 Degrees   45 Minutes

1) 2 (15 ounce) cans hominy, drained
2) 1 cup chopped onion
3) 2 cups grated cheddar cheese
4) 1 (15 ounce) can chili or enchilada sauce

Place hominy and onions in casserole. Top with 1/2 of cheese. Spread chili over top and then remainder of the cheese. Bake. Serves 4 to 6.

Sunday Pot Roast

Bake 350 Degrees   4 Hours

1) 4 to 6 pound chuck roast
2) 1 package dry onion soup mix
3) 1 can cream of mushroom soup
4) 4 to 6 medium potatoes, peeled and quartered

Place roast on large sheet of heavy duty foil. Mix soups and cover roast with soup mixture. Add potatoes and bring foil up and over roast. Roll and secure edges tightly, about 6 inches above roast. Bake. Serves 8 to 10.

New York Roast Beef

Bake 350 Degrees   20 Minutes per Pound

1)   6 to 7 pound eye of round
2)   1 tablespoon oil
3)   1/2 teaspoon garlic powder
4)   1 teaspoon ground oregano

Rub oil all over roast. Combine garlic and oregano and rub over the oiled roast. Place in shallow baking pan with fat side up. Bake. Serves 10 to 12.

Flank Steak Joy

Broil   8-10 Minutes per Side

1)   2 pounds lean flank steak
2)   2 tablespoons soy sauce
3)   1 tablespoon sherry
4)   1 teaspoon honey

Mix soy, sherry and honey and marinate meat 4 hours or longer. Remove the steak from marinade and place on broiler pan. Broil. Slice across the grain into thin strips and serve. Serves 6 to 8.

Marinated Flank Steak

Broil   8-10 Minutes per Side

1)   2 pounds flank steak
2)   1 (8 ounce) bottle Italian salad dressing
3)   Salt to taste (optional)
4)   Pepper to taste (optional)

Pour dressing over steak and marinate for 4 hours or longer. Salt and pepper if desired. Broil. Slice across grain in thin strips. Serves 6 to 8.

Terriyake Marinade

Broil   8-10 Minutes each Side

1)   2 pounds flank steak
2)   1/3 cup soy sauce
3)   1/3 cup pineapple juice
4)   1/3 cup red wine

Combine soy, pineapple and wine. Pour over flank steak and marinate 4 hours or longer. Broil. Serves 6 to 8.

Sherried Beef

Bake 250 Degrees   3 Hours

1)   3 pounds lean beef, cubed in 1 1/2 inch cubes
2)   2 cans cream of mushroom soup
3)   1/2 cup cooking sherry
4)   1/2 package dry onion soup mix

Mix all ingredients in casserole and bake covered. Serve over rice or egg noodles. Serves 8.

Round Steak Bake

Bake 350 Degrees   1 1/2 Hours

1)   2 pounds round steak
2)   4 large potatoes, peeled and quartered
3)   2 (6 ounce) cans mushrooms, undrained
4)   1 package dry onion soup mix

Place steak on foil and sprinkle soup mix on steak. Place potatoes evenly over steak and pour mushrooms with liquid over potatoes and steak. Wrap foil tightly. Bake. Serves 4 to 6.

Beef Stroganoff

Stove Top

1)   1 1/2 pounds round steak, cut in 1/4 inch strips
2)   2 tablespoons onion soup mix
3)   1 (6 ounce) can sliced mushrooms
4)   1 cup sour cream

Brown round steak in skillet. Add soup mix and can of mushrooms with liquid. Heat until bubbly. Slowly add sour cream and cook until thoroughly heated. Serve with noodles. Serves 4 to 6.

Swiss Steak

Stove Top   1 1/2 Hours

1)   2 pounds round steak
2)   1/2 cup flour
3)   1 tablespoon oil
4)   2 (14 1/2 ounce) cans stewed tomatoes

Flour steak and brown in oil. Remove from skillet and drain oil. Pour 1 can of tomatoes in skillet. Place steak on top and pour remaining can of tomatoes on steak. Cover and simmer. Serve with mashed potatoes. Serves 4 to 6.

Beef in Wine Sauce

Stove Top   2 Hours

1)   3 pounds sirloin steak, cut in 1/4 inch strips
2)   2 tablespoons flour
3)   2 cans creamy onion soup
4)   2 cups Burgundy wine

Season meat to taste. Dredge strips in flour and brown in skillet. Add wine and soup and stir. Simmer covered. Serve with noodles. Serves 6 to 8.

Beef Goulash

Bake 350 Degrees   1 Hour

1)   2 pounds stew beef
2)   1 tablespoon oil
3)   1 1/2 cups chopped onion
4)   1 can zesty tomato soup

Saute meat and onion in oil. Add soup. Cover and place in oven. Bake. Serve with noodles. Serves 4 to 6.

Hot Dog Stew

Stove Top   25 Minutes

1)   1 package beef hot dogs, cut in 1/2 inch pieces
2)   3 medium potatoes, peeled and diced
3)   2 tablespoons flour
4)   1/2 cup water

Brown hot dogs in ungreased skillet. Add diced potatoes. Mix flour
and water until smooth. Pour over hot dog and potato mixture.
Salt and pepper to taste. Cover and simmer. Serves 4.

New England Dinner

3 Hours   Stove Top

1)   4 pounds corned beef
2)   1 head cabbage, cut into eighths
3)   8 potatoes, peeled and halved
4)   8 carrots, peeled and halved

Cover meat with cold water. Simmer 3 hours, adding the potatoes,
carrots and cabbage the last hour. Drain and serve. Serves 8 to 10.

Liver with Apples and Onions

Stove Top

1)   4 slices calf liver (about 1 pound)
2)   4 tablespoons margarine
3)   3 medium onions, peeled and sliced
4)   2 apples, cored and cut into 1/2 inch thick rings

Dry the liver. Saute onions in 3 tablespoons margarine. Remove onion rings and saute apples until they are cooked through but not mushy (about 2 to 3 minutes on each side). Remove apples. Saute liver about 2 to 3 minutes on each side. Place on platter and top with onions and apples. Serves 4.

Sherry Chicken

Bake 350 Degrees   1 Hour

1)   6 medium chicken breasts, skinned and boned
2)   1 can cream of mushroom soup
3)   1 1/3 cups sour cream
4)   1/2 cup cooking sherry

Place chicken in greased baking dish. Combine remaining ingredients and pour over chicken. Bake. Serves 4 to 6.

Company Chicken

Bake 350 Degrees   1 Hour

1)   6 chicken breasts, skinned and boned
2)   1/4 cup sherry or white wine
3)   1/2 cup chicken broth
4)   1/2 cup grated parmesan cheese

Place chicken in baking dish. Pour wine and broth on top of chicken. Sprinkle with parmesan cheese. Bake covered 45 minutes and uncovered 15 minutes. Serve with white rice. Serves 4 to 6.

Soy Sauce Chicken

Bake 350 Degrees   1 Hour

1)   4 chicken breasts, skinned and boned
2)   1 cup sour cream
3)   1/4 cup soy sauce
4)   1/4 teaspoon black pepper (optional)

Place chicken in greased casserole dish. Mix sour cream, soy sauce and black pepper (optional) together. Spread over chicken. Bake covered. Serves 4.

Chicken Dried Beef I

Bake 300 Degrees   2 Hours

1)   6 chicken breasts, skinned and boned
2)   2 (4 ounce) jars sliced dried beef, separated
3)   6 strips bacon
4)   1 can cream of mushroom soup

Place dried beef in greased casserole. Wrap bacon strip around each chicken breast and place over beef. Spread soup over chicken; cover and bake. Serves 4 to 6.

Chicken Dried Beef II

Bake 275 Degrees   2 Hours

1)   1 (4 ounce) jar sliced dried beef, chopped
2)   4 chicken breasts, skinned and boned
3)   1 cup sour cream
4)   1 can cream of mushroom soup

Place dried beef in bottom of greased casserole and place chicken on top. Combine sour cream and soup; spread over chicken. Bake uncovered. Serves 4.

Chicken Oregano

Bake 325 Degrees   1 1/2 Hours

1)   4 chicken breasts, skinned and boned
2)   1 tablespoon oregano
3)   1 teaspoon garlic salt
4)   1/2 cup margarine, melted

Mix all ingredients except chicken. Pour over chicken and marinate at least 4 hours. Bake uncovered. Serves 4.

Chicken Supreme

Bake 300 Degrees   **1 1/2 Hours**

1)   4 chicken breasts, skinned and boned
2)   4 slices onion
3)   4 to 5 potatoes, peeled and quartered
4)   1 can golden mushroom soup

Line casserole with foil. Place chicken on foil. Top chicken with onion and place potatoes around chicken. Pour soup over potatoes and chicken. Seal foil tightly over chicken. Bake. Serves 4.

Oven Fried Ritz Chicken

Bake 350 Degrees   **1 Hour**

1)   8 chicken breasts, skinned and boned
2)   1/2 box Ritz crackers, crushed into fine crumbs
3)   1/2 cup yogurt
4)   1/4 teaspoon pepper

Dip chicken in yogurt and roll in cracker crumbs with pepper. Place chicken in casserole dish and bake 30 minutes on each side. Serves 6 to 8.

Baked Chicken Parmesan

Bake 350 Degrees   **1 Hour**

1)   3 pounds chicken pieces
2)   1 cup cornflake crumbs
3)   1/2 cup grated parmesan cheese
4)   3/4 cup Miracle Whip salad dressing

Combine crumbs and cheese. Brush chicken with salad dressing and coat with crumb mixture. Place in casserole dish and bake. Serves 4 to 6.

Potato Chip Chicken

Bake 350 Degrees   1 Hour

1)   2 to 3 pounds chicken pieces, remove skin
2)   1 cup margarine, melted
3)   2 cups crushed potato chips
4)   1/4 teaspoon garlic salt

Mix crushed potato chips with garlic salt (flavored chips such as sour cream-onion can be used). Dip chicken in melted margarine and roll in potato chips. Place on baking sheet. Pour remaining margarine and chips over chicken. Bake. Serves 4 to 6.

Chicken Scallop

Bake 350 Degrees   30 Minutes

1)   1 1/2 cups diced cooked chicken
2)   1 (6 ounce) package noodles
3)   2 cups chicken gravy (see recipe below)
4)   1/2 cup buttered bread crumbs

Boil noodles, drain. Arrange alternate layers of noodles and chicken and gravy in greased baking dish. Cover with crumbs and bake. Serves 4.

Quick Chicken Gravy

1)   1 1/2 tablespoons flour
2)   1 cup milk
3)   1 can cream of chicken soup
4)   1/4 teaspoon pepper

Blend flour and milk and add to soup. Season with pepper if desired. Heat slowly to boiling and cook until thickened.

Chicken Dressing

Bake 350 Degrees   45 Minutes

1)   1 chicken
2)   1 (8 ounce) package corn bread stuffing mix
3)   2 cans cream of chicken mushroom soup
4)   1/2 cup margarine, melted

Boil chicken until meat separates from bone. Cool and debone. Retain 2 cups of broth. Mix melted margarine with stuffing mix. Dilute soup with 1 cup broth. Layer in large baking dish — beginning with dressing, then chicken, then soup. Repeat ending with dressing. Pour remaining 1 cup of broth over mixture. Bake uncovered. Serves 4 to 6.

Chicken Rice

Bake 350 Degrees   30 Minutes

1)   2 cups cooked chicken, cut up
2)   1 box Uncle Ben's Wild Rice Mix
3)   1 can cream mushroom soup
4)   1/2 soup can milk

Mix all ingredients and pour in greased 2-quart dish. Cover and bake. Serves 4 to 6.

Busy Day Chicken

Bake 325 Degrees   2 Hours

1)   2 to 3 pounds chicken pieces
2)   1 cup rice, uncooked
3)   1 package dry onion soup mix
4)   1 can cream of celery soup

Place rice in greased casserole with chicken on top. Sprinkle with onion soup. Mix celery soup and two cans water; pour over the above. Bake covered. Serves 4 to 6.

Chicken Dijon

Bake 350 Degrees   1 Hour

1)   3 pounds chicken pieces
2)   1/2 cup Miracle Whip salad dressing
3)   1/4 cup Dijon mustard
4)   1 1/4 cups dry bread crumbs

Combine salad dressing and mustard. Coat chicken with mixture and crumbs. Bake. Serves 4 to 6.

Chicken Sour Cream

Bake 350 Degrees   1 1/2 Hours

1)   3 pounds chicken fryer, cut up
2)   1 (8 ounce) carton sour cream
3)   1 package dry onion soup mix
4)   1/2 cup milk

Mix sour cream, soup and milk and pour over chicken. Cover and bake. Serves 4 to 6.

Sweet and Sour Chicken

Bake 350 Degrees   **1 1/2 Hours**

1)   2 to 3 pounds chicken pieces
2)   1 package dry onion soup mix
3)   1 (12 ounce) jar apricot preserves
4)   1 (8 ounce) bottle Russian salad dressing

Place chicken in shallow baking pan. Mix remaining ingredients and pour on chicken. Bake. Serve with white rice. Serves 4 to 6.

Lemon Butter Chicken

Bake 350 Degrees   **1 1/2 Hours**

1)   2 to 3 pound chicken pieces
2)   1/2 cup margarine, melted
3)   2 lemons
4)   1/2 teaspoon garlic salt

Rub chicken with lemon. Mix margarine, juice of one lemon and garlic salt. Pour over chicken and bake. Baste occasionally. Serves 4 to 6.

Chicken-Chicken Soup

Bake 350 Degrees   **1 1/2 Hours**

1)   2 to 3 pounds chicken pieces
2)   2 cans mushroom chicken soup
3)   1/2 cup milk
4)   Parsley

Place chicken in large casserole. Mix soup and milk. Pour over chicken. Sprinkle with parsley. Bake. Serves 4 to 6.

Golden Chicken

Bake 400 Degrees   1 Hour

1)   2 pounds chicken pieces
2)   2 tablespoons margarine
3)   1 can cream of chicken soup
4)   1/2 cup sliced almonds

Melt margarine in 9x13-inch baking dish. Arrange chicken in dish; bake for 40 minutes. Turn chicken and cover with soup. Sprinkle with almonds and bake 20 minutes longer. Serves 4 to 6.

Orange Chicken

Bake 350 Degrees   1 Hour 15 Minutes

1)   8 pieces of chicken
2)   1 cup flour
3)   1 can frozen orange juice, thawed
4)   1 bunch green onions, chopped

Dredge chicken pieces in flour; brown. Place in casserole. Cover with green onions and drizzle with juice. Cover and bake 1 hour; uncover and continue to bake for 15 minutes. Serves 4 to 6.

Worcestershire Chicken

Bake 350 Degrees   1 Hour

1)   2 to 3 pounds chicken pieces
2)   1/4 cup Worcestershire sauce
3)   1/2 cup margarine
4)   2 tablespoons lemon pepper

Place chicken in large greased casserole. Spread margarine on each piece of chicken. Sprinkle with lemon pepper and Worcestershire sauce. Bake. Serves 4 to 6.

Mushroom Chicken

Bake 350 Degrees   1 1/2 Hours

1)   6 chicken breasts, thighs or legs
2)   3 tablespoons oil
3)   2 (4 ounce) cans button mushrooms
4)   2 cans cream of mushroom soup

Brown chicken in oil in frying pan. Remove and arrange chicken in casserole. Combine soup and mushrooms and pour over chicken. Bake. Serves 4 to 6.

Lemon Pepper Chicken

Bake 350 Degrees   1 Hour

1)   2 to 3 pounds chicken pieces
2)   4 tablespoons margarine, melted
3)   1/2 cup soy sauce
4)   Lemon pepper

Place chicken in greased baking dish. Spread margarine, soy sauce and lemon pepper on each piece of chicken. Bake. Serves 4 to 6.

Marinated Chicken

Broil   40 Minutes

1)   2 broiling chickens
2)   3/4 cup olive oil
3)   1 clove garlic, finely chopped
4)   1/2 cup chopped parsley

Split chicken down the back. Combine oil, garlic and parsley; marinate chicken for minimum of 1/2 hour or overnight. Arrange marinated chickens, skin side up, on preheated broiler 5 inches from heat. Broil 20 minutes per side. Baste regularly. Serves 6 to 8.

Italian Broiled Chicken

Broil   16 Minutes
Bake 350 Degrees   20 Minutes

1)   1 fryer chicken, quartered
2)   1/2 cup margarine
3)   3 tablespoons lemon juice
4)   1 package Italian salad dressing mix

Melt margarine in frying pan and add lemon juice and salad mix. Dip chicken in this mixture and place, skin side up, on rack in broiler pan. Broil 8 minutes per side. Change oven setting to 350 degrees and pour remaining butter mixture over chicken. Bake uncovered at 350 degrees for 20 minutes. Serves 4 to 6.

Chicken Cacciatore

Stove Top

1) 2 1/2 pounds chicken pieces
2) 1 medium onion, chopped
3) 1 (14 ounce) jar spaghetti sauce
4) 1/2 teaspoon dried basil

Brown chicken pieces skin side down over low heat. Cook chicken 10 minutes each side. Saute onions until soft. Stir in sauce and basil. Cover and simmer 20 minutes. Serve with spaghetti. Serves 4 to 6.

Chicken Livers and Mushrooms

Stove Top

1) 1 pound chicken livers
2) 2 tablespoons oil
3) 1 (6 ounce) large can whole mushrooms
4) 1/2 cup red wine

Saute livers slowly in oil. Add red wine and mushrooms. Heat. Serve over rice. Serves 4.

Swinging Wings

Bake 350 Degrees   1 Hour

1) 10 chicken wings
2) 1/2 cup margarine, melted
3) 1 small box parmesan cheese
4) 1 teaspoon garlic powder

Dip wings in margarine and then in combined mixture of cheese and garlic powder. Place in casserole and bake. Serves 4.

Cornish Hens

Bake 350 Degrees   1 Hour

1) 4 Cornish hens
2) 4 tablespoons margarine
3) 1/2 cup water
4) 2 tablespoons soy sauce

Rub hens with margarine. Place in greased baking dish and spoon water and soy sauce mixture over hens. Cover with foil and bake for 45 minutes. Remove cover and bake 15 minutes longer. Serves 4.

Sweet Sour Pork Chops

Bake 350 Degrees   1 Hour

1)   6 to 8 thick pork chops
2)   1/4 cup soy sauce
3)   1/4 cup chili sauce
4)   1/4 cup honey

Mix honey, soy, and chili sauces. Place pork chops in greased 3-quart casserole. Pour mixture over chops. Bake. Serves 6 to 8.

Hawaiian Pork Chops

Stove Top   1 1/2 Hours

1)   4 loin pork chops
2)   1/4 cup flour
3)   2 tablespoons oil
4)   4 slices canned pineapple (reserve 1/3 cup juice)

Dredge chops in flour. Brown in skillet with oil. Top each chop with a ring of pineapple. Add pineapple juice. Cover and cook slowly. Remove meat and pineapple to platter. Pour the remaining juice over chops. Serves 4.

Hawaiian Baked Pork

Bake 350 Degrees   **1 Hour**
Bake 450 Degrees   **10 Minutes**

1)   4 pork chops
2)   2 cups crushed pineapple
3)   3 medium sweet potatoes, peeled and sliced
4)   2 tablespoons brown sugar

Place pineapple with juice in large greased baking dish. Place sliced sweet potatoes over pineapple and sprinkle with brown sugar. Place pork chops on top of sweet potatoes. Bake covered 350 degrees; uncovered 450 degrees. Serves 4.

Pork Chop Scallop

Stove Top   **45 Minutes**

1)   4 (1/2 inch thick) pork chops
2)   1 package scalloped potatoes
3)   2 tablespoons margarine
4)   Milk (as called for in box of potatoes)

In skillet brown chops in margarine. Remove chops and set aside. Empty potatoes and packet of seasoned sauce mix into skillet. Stir in water and milk called for on package. Heat to boiling, reduce heat and place chops on top. Cover and simmer 35 minutes or until potatoes are tender and chops are thoroughly done. Serves 4.

Pork Potato Casserole

| Bake 350 Degrees | 1 Hour |
| Bake 375 Degrees | 1/2 Hour |

1) 4 to 6 pork chops
2) 4 to 5 potatoes, peeled and cut in 1/2 inch slices
3) 1 can cheddar cheese soup
4) 1/2 can milk

Place two layers of potatoes in bottom of a greased casserole dish. Place pork chops on top. Combine soup and milk. Pour over chops. Bake covered 350 degrees; uncovered 375 degrees. Serves 4 to 6.

Sausage Casserole

| Bake 400 Degrees | 25 Minutes |

1) 1 pound bulk pork sausage
2) 2 (15 ounce) cans beans with spicy sauce
3) 1 (14 1/2 ounce) can whole tomatoes, drained
4) 1 package corn muffin mix

Brown sausage, drain fat. Add beans and tomatoes and blend. Bring to a boil. Pour into a 2 1/2-quart greased casserole. Prepare muffin mix according to package. Drop by spoonfuls over meat and bean mixture. Bake 25 minutes or until top is browned. Serves 4 to 6.

Quickie Hawaiian Pork

Stove Top   1 Hour

1)   2 pound lean pork roast, cut in 1 inch cubes)
2)   1 (14 ounce) can pineapple chunks with juice
3)   1/4 cup vinegar
4)   1 teaspoon ginger

Combine meat, pineapple with juice, vinegar and ginger. Simmer 1 hour covered. Serve over rice. Serves 6.

Roast Pork in Marinade

Bake 350 Degrees   4 Hours

1)   4 to 6 pound lean pork roast
2)   1 (15 ounce) can tomatoes, chopped
3)   1/4 cup white vinegar
4)   1/4 cup water

Place roast in roasting pan. Mix and pour the remaining ingredients over roast. Best marinated overnight. Cover and bake. Serves 8 to 10.

Sunday Ham

Bake 300 Degrees   3 Hours

1)   2 to 3 pounds boneless smoked ham
2)   1/4 cup prepared mustard
3)   1/4 cup brown sugar
4)   4 potatoes, peeled and quartered

Place ham in roaster. Combine mustard and sugar. Spread over ham. Place potatoes around ham. Cover and bake. Serves 8 to 10.

Pork Casserole

Bake 325 Degrees   4 Hours

1) 2 pounds lean pork, cut into 1 inch cubes
2) 2 (16 ounce) large cans sauerkraut, drained
3) 2 medium onions, sliced
4) 3 cups water

Brown pork in skillet and set aside. Spread 1/2 of sauerkraut in a 2-quart greased casserole. Cover with 1 onion. Place pork on top. Layer onions and sauerkraut on top of pork. Pour water over all, cover and bake. Serves 6.

Spareribs Sauerkraut

Bake 350 Degrees   1 Hour

1) 4 pounds spareribs
2) 2 (16 ounce) large cans sauerkraut
3) 1/4 cup brown sugar
4) 1/2 cup hot water

Place sauerkraut in greased casserole and sprinkle with brown sugar. Place spareribs on sauerkraut. Add hot water, cover and bake. Serves 4.

Barbecued Spareribs

Bake 350 Degrees   2 Hours

1) 4 pounds spareribs
2) 2 medium onions, sliced
3) 1 (18 ounce) bottle barbecue sauce
4) 1 teaspoon brown sugar (optional)

Place ribs in roaster. Add onions and brown sugar (optional). Pour sauce over ribs and cook covered for 1 1/2 hours. Remove cover and cook 30 minutes longer. Serves 4.

Pork Tenderloin

Bake 325 Degrees   5 Hours

1) 3 pounds pork tenderloin
2) 1 (15 ounce) can tomato sauce
3) 1 package dry onion soup mix
4) 2 tablespoons Worcestershire sauce

Place tenderloin strips on aluminum foil. Mix remaining ingredients; spread over meat. Seal foil and place in shallow pan. Bake. Cut meat into 1-inch slices. Pour gravy in pan over slices of meat. Serves 6 to 8.

Cranberry Ham

Bake 300 Degrees   1 Hour

1) 1 (2-inch thick) slice ham
2) 1 cup whole cranberry sauce
3) 2 tablespoons brown sugar
4) 1/4 teaspoon cloves

Place ham in greased casserole. Spoon cranberry sauce evenly over ham. Sprinkle with brown sugar and cloves. Bake covered. Serves 4.

Cheesy Fillets

Bake 500 Degrees   12 Minutes

1)   **2 pounds fish fillets**
2)   **1/2 cup French dressing**
3)   **1 1/2 cups crushed cheese crackers**
4)   **2 tablespoons margarine, melted**

Cut fish into serving portions. Dip into dressing and roll in cracker crumbs. Place on greased cookie sheet and drizzle margarine over fish. Bake. Serves 4.

Fish Delight

Bake 350 Degrees   20 Minutes
Broil   10 Minutes

1)   **4 fish fillets**
2)   **1/4 cup soy sauce**
3)   **1/4 cup lemon juice**
4)   **1/2 teaspoon sugar or ginger (optional)**

Place fillets in greased casserole dish. Mix soy sauce and lemon juice with sugar or ginger if desired. Pour over fish. Bake and then place under broiler. Serves 2 to 4.

Chipper Trout

Bake 500 Degrees   15 Minutes

1)   2 pounds Gulf trout or other fresh fillets
2)   1/2 cup Caesar salad dressing
3)   1 cup crushed potato chips
4)   1/2 cup grated sharp cheddar cheese

Dip fillets in salad dressing and place in greased casserole dish. Combine chips and cheese and sprinkle over fillets. Bake. Serves 4.

Crunchy Baked Fish

Bake 500 Degrees   15 Minutes

1)   1 pound fish fillets
2)   1 cup party mix, crushed into fine crumbs
3)   1/2 cup low fat yogurt
4)   Sprinkle parmesan cheese (optional)

Dip fillets into yogurt and then into the crushed party mix crumbs. Sprinkle with cheese if desired. Arrange in single layer in greased baking dish. Bake. Serves 2 to 4.

Barbecued Trout

Bake 350 Degrees   20 Minutes

1)   4 trout
2)   4 tablespoons minced onion
3)   1 cup barbecue sauce
4)   Salt and pepper

Place onion, barbecue sauce in body cavity of trout. Salt and pepper to taste. Wrap trout individually in foil and bake. Serves 4.

Broiled Trout

Broil   13 Minutes

1) 2 pounds fish fillets
2) 2 tablespoons grated onion
3) 2 large tomatoes, cut into small pieces
4) 1 cup grated Swiss cheese

Place fillets in greased casserole. Sprinkle onion and tomatoes over fillets. Broil 10 minutes. Sprinkle with cheese and broil another 3 minutes. Serves 4.

Tuna Chip Casserole

Bake 375 Degrees   30 Minutes

1) 1 (6 1/2 ounce) can tuna, drained
2) 1 (10 3/4 ounce) can cream of mushroom soup
3) 3/4 cup milk
4) 1 cup crushed potato chips

Break chunks of tuna into a bowl. Stir in soup and milk. Add 3/4 cup crushed potato chips. Mix well. Pour into greased baking dish. Sprinkle the remaining chips over top. Bake. Serves 4 to 6.

Herbed Salmon Steaks

Bake 450 Degrees   45 Minutes

1)   3 (12 ounce) packages frozen salmon steaks
2)   1/4 cup lemon juice
3)   2 teaspoons marjoram leaves
4)   2 teaspoons onion salt

Place frozen fish in greased casserole. Mix lemon juice, marjoram leaves and onion salt. Spoon on fish and bake. Serves 4 to 6.

Salmonettes

Stove Top

1)   1 (15 ounce) can pink salmon, drained and flaked
2)   1 egg
3)   1/2 cup biscuit mix
4)   1/2 cup oil

Mix salmon and egg in bowl. Add biscuit mix and stir. Heat oil in skillet and drop salmon mixture by tablespoonfuls into skillet. Flatten each salmonette with spatula. Cook each side until brown, around 2 to 3 minutes per side. Serves 4.

Serving Idea: Lemon Butter Sauce is complimentary to many hot fish entrees. To make, cream 1/2 cup softened butter and gradually add 3 tablespoons lemon juice.

Scalloped Oysters

Bake 350 Degrees

1) 1 pint oysters
2) 2 cups fine cracker crumbs
3) 4 tablespoons margarine
4) 1 can condensed chicken gumbo soup

Drain and reserve liquid from oysters. Place one layer oysters in large baking dish; season to taste and cover with layer of crumbs and half of soup mixture. Repeat layers. Dot with margarine and bake until edges of oysters curl and top is browned. Serves 4.

Italian Shrimp

Stove Top   10 Minutes

1) 3 pounds raw shrimp, peeled and cleaned
2) 1/2 pound margarine
3) 12 ounces Italian dressing
4) Juice of 2 lemons

Melt margarine and mix dressing and lemon juice in skillet. Stir in shrimp. Saute for 10 minutes, turning occasionally. Serves 4 to 6.

Scallops and Bacon

Bake 475 Degrees   20 Minutes

1)   1 pound scallops
2)   3 tablespoons margarine
3)   8 slices bacon
4)   Salt and pepper

Cook scallops in margarine 5 minutes. Cut bacon into 2-inch pieces. Arrange bacon and scallops alternately on skewer. Sprinkle with salt and pepper. To bake, insert skewers in uncooked potato halves, so they will stand upright. Bake. Serves 4.

Fish Roll

Bake 400 Degrees   30 Minutes

1)   1 (6 ounce) can crab
2)   1 can refrigerator biscuits
3)   1 small onion, chopped
4)   Mayonnaise

Roll biscuit dough to 1/4-inch thick on floured board. Combine fish and onion and moisten slightly with mayonnaise. Mix and spread on dough. Roll this dough and mixture into a jelly roll and cut into 1 1/2-inch slices. Bake on greased baking sheet. Serves 4 to 6.

Crabmeat Casserole

Bake 350 Degrees   30 Minutes

1) 1 pound crabmeat or imitation crabmeat
2) 1 (2.8 ounce) can Durkees fried onions
3) 1 can cream of mushroom soup
4) 3/4 cup cracker crumbs

Mix all ingredients. Place in buttered casserole dish. Bake. Serves 4 to 6.

Seafood Casserole

Bake 400 Degrees   30 Minutes

1) 1/4 pound crabmeat, flaked
2) 1/4 pound shrimp, peeled and cleaned
3) 1/4 pound scallops
4) 1 can cheddar cheese soup

Mix fish ingredients and place in greased casserole dish. Cover with soup and bake. Serve with rice. Serves 4.

Desserts

Pie Shell

1) 1 cup flour
2) 1/2 teaspoon salt
3) 1/3 cup shortening
4) 2 to 3 tablespoons ice water

Combine flour and salt. Cut shortening into dry ingredients until mixture resembles corn meal. Add ice water 1 tablespoon at a time. Stir with fork. Form into a ball. Place on lightly floured surface and roll from center to edge until 1/8-inch thick. Makes one 9-inch pie shell.

Pat-in-Pan Crust

1) 2 cups flour
2) 2/3 cup margarine
3) 1/2 cup chopped nuts (almonds or pecans)
4) 1/2 cup powdered sugar

Mix ingredients. Press firmly into ungreased pie plate. Makes two 9-inch pie shells. Bake 15 minutes at 350 degrees.

Nut Crust

1) 1/4 cup margarine, softened
2) 1/4 cup sugar
3) 1 tablespoon flour
4) 1 cup pecans, ground

Combine all ingredients. Press over bottom and sides of greased 9-inch pie plate. Bake 10 minutes at 325 degrees. Cool.

Graham Cracker Crust

1) 1 1/2 cups graham cracker crumbs
2) 2 tablespoons sugar
3) 6 tablespoons margarine, melted
4) Sprinkle of cinnamon (optional)

Combine all ingredients and press evenly into a 9-inch pie plate. Bake 10 minutes at 350 degrees. Cool.

Chocolate Pie Shell

1) 1 1/4 cups chocolate wafer crumbs
2) 1/4 cup margarine, melted
3) 2 tablespoons sugar
4) 1/4 teaspoon cinnamon

Combine all ingredients and press onto bottom of greased 9-inch pie plate. Bake 8 minutes at 375 degrees.

Meringue Shell

1) 4 egg whites, room temperature
2) 1/2 teaspoon cream of tartar
3) 1 1/2 cups sugar
4) 1 teaspoon vanilla

Beat egg whites until foamy. Add cream of tartar and beat until stiff. Gradually add sugar and vanilla. Fully shape in greased 9-inch pie plate. Bake 1 hour at 275 degrees. Let cool in oven. Great for fruit or cream fillings.

Apple Cream Pie
Unbaked Pie Shell

1) 4 cups apples, peeled and diced
2) 1 cup sugar
3) 1 cup half and half
4) 2 tablespoons flour

Combine all ingredients. Pour into unbaked pie shell. Bake 45 minutes to 1 hour or until brown at 350 degrees.

Bourbon Pie
Baked Chocolate Pie Shell

1) 21 large marshmallows
2) 1 (12 ounce) can evaporated milk
3) 1 cup whipping cream, whipped
4) 3 tablespoons bourbon

Combine marshmallows and canned milk in saucepan. Cook over low heat, stirring constantly, until all the marshmallows have melted. Chill completely. Whip cream and fold in marshmallow mixture and bourbon. Pour into pie shell and chill 4 to 6 hours.

Coconut Pie
Unbaked Pie Shell

1) 3 eggs
2) 1/4 cup buttermilk
3) 2/3 cup butter, melted
4) 2 cups (7 ounces) flaked coconut

Mix all ingredients and pour into pie shell. Bake 45 minutes at 350 degrees.

Caramel Box Pie
Baked Nut Crust

1)   1 (14 ounce) can sweetened condensed milk
2)   1 large banana, peeled and sliced
3)   1 (8 ounce) carton Cool Whip
4)   2 (1.4 ounce) Skor bars, chilled and crushed

Place a non-stick skillet over medium-low heat and add sweetened condensed milk. Cook for 10 to 12 minutes, stirring frequently. Milk will thicken and turn caramel color. Remove from heat. Cool. Place sliced bananas in 9-inch nut crust and spread caramelized milk over bananas. Spoon Cool Whip on top and sprinkle with crushed candy. Refrigerate.

Quick Cheese Cake Pie
Graham Cracker Crust

1)   1 (8 ounce) package cream cheese, softened
2)   2 cups whole milk
3)   1 (3 1/2 ounce) package lemon instant pudding mix
4)   Cool Whip topping (optional)

Blend softened cream cheese and 1/2 cup of the milk. Add remaining milk and pudding mix. Beat slowly just until well mixed, about 1 minute...do not over beat! Pour at once into graham cracker crust. Chill 1 hour. Serve topped with Cool Whip if desired.

Cheesecake
Unbaked Graham Cracker Crust

1) 3 (8 ounce) packages cream cheese
2) 1 cup sugar
3) 5 eggs
4) 1 1/2 teaspoons vanilla

Cream the cream cheese and eggs by adding one egg at a time. Add sugar and vanilla. Pour into graham cracker crust and bake 1 hour at 350 degrees, or until center is set.

Lazy Chocolate Icebox Pie
Baked Pie Shell

1) 20 large marshmallows
2) 1 (8 ounce) almond chocolate bar
3) 1 (8 ounce) carton Cool Whip
4) Sprinkle finely chopped pecans (optional)

Melt marshmallows and chocolate over low heat or double boiler. Cool partially and fold in Cool Whip. Sprinkle with pecans if desired. Place in pie shell. Chill.

Lemonade Pie
Baked Graham Cracker Crust

1) 1 (14 ounce) can sweetened condensed milk
2) 1 (6 ounce) can frozen lemonade, thawed
3) 1 (8 ounce) carton Cool Whip
4) Sprinkle graham cracker crumbs (optional)

Combine and mix all ingredients. Do not beat. Place in pie shell. Sprinkle with crumbs if desired and freeze.

Cookie Cream Pie

Baked Chocolate Pie Shell

1) 1 1/2 cups cold half and half
2) 1 (3 1/2 ounce) package instant vanilla pudding
3) 1 (8 ounce) carton Cool Whip
4) 1 cup crushed chocolate sandwich cookies

Pour half and half into large bowl. Add pudding mix. Beat at low speed until well blended, about 1 minute. Let stand 5 minutes. Fold in Cool Whip and crushed cookies. Pour into baked pie shell. Freeze about 6 hours. Remove and let stand 10 minutes before serving.

Mississippi Mud Pie

Baked Chocolate Pie Shell

1) 1 1/2 cups half and half
2) 1 (3 1/2 ounce) package instant vanilla pudding
3) 1 tablespoon instant coffee
4) 1 (8 ounce) carton Cool Whip

Pour half and half into large bowl. Add pudding mix. Beat at low speed until well blended, about 1 minute. Let stand 5 minutes and fold in instant coffee and Cool Whip. Place in pie shell. Freeze about 6 hours. Remove and let stand 10 minutes before serving.

Millionaire Pie

Baked Pie Shell

1) 1 cup sugar
2) 1 (8 ounce) package cream cheese, softened
3) 1 (15 1/4 ounce) can crushed pineapple, drained
4) 1 (8 ounce) carton Cool Whip

Cream sugar with the cream cheese. Add drained pineapple. Fold in Cool Whip until well blended. Place in pie shell. Refrigerate. Serve cold.

Peach Pie

Baked Pie Shell

1) 7 peaches, peeled and sliced
2) 1/4 cup sugar
3) 2 tablespoons cornstarch
4) 2 tablespoons margarine

Place all ingredients in pan and cook on stove top until thick and clear. Cool. Place in pie shell. Refrigerate.

Pineapple Pie

Baked Graham Cracker Crust

1) 1 (14 ounce) can sweetened condensed milk
2) 1/2 cup lemon juice
3) 1 (20 ounce) can crushed pineapple, drained
4) 1 (8 ounce) carton Cool Whip

Combine milk and lemon juice. Stir well. Fold in pineapple and Cool Whip. Spoon into graham cracker crust. Chill.

Peach Yogurt Pie
Baked Graham Cracker Crust

1) 1 (8 3/4 ounce) can sliced peaches
2) 2 (8 ounce) containers fruit flavored yogurt
3) 1 (8 ounce) carton Cool Whip
4) Sprinkle graham cracker crumbs (optional)

Combine fruit and yogurt, then fold in Cool Whip, blending well. Spoon into graham cracker crust. Sprinkle with crumbs if deisred. Freeze until firm, about 4 hours. Remove from freezer and place in refrigerator 30 minutes before serving.

Pecan Pie
Unbaked Pie Shell

1) 3 eggs, beaten
2) 1 cup sugar
3) 3/4 cup white corn syrup
4) 1 cup chopped pecans

Mix all ingredients and place in pie shell. Bake 1 hour at 325 degrees or until inserted knife comes out clean.

Cocktail Pie
Baked Meringue Shell

1) 2 cups sour cream
2) 1/2 cup sugar
3) 1 teaspoon vanilla
4) 1 (30 ounce) can fruit cocktail, well drained

Combine sour cream, sugar and vanilla. Fold in drained fruit cocktail. Place in cooled meringue shell. Refrigerate.

Pumpkin Pie

Unbaked Pie Shell

1) 1 (16 ounce) can pumpkin
2) 1 (12 ounce) can sweetened condensed milk
3) 2 eggs
4) 1 teaspoon pumpkin pie spice

Combine all ingredients and mix well. Pour into pie shell. Bake 15 minutes at 425 degrees; then reduce heat and bake 35 to 40 minutes longer at 350 degrees.

Strawberry Pie

Baked Graham Cracker Crust

1) 1 (3 ounce) box strawberry Jello
2) 2/3 cup boiling water and 2 cups ice cubes
3) 1 (8 ounce) carton Cool Whip
4) 1 cup sliced strawberries

Dissolve Jello in boiling water. Stir Jello about 3 minutes; add 2 cups ice cubes. Stir until ice melts and Jello thickens. Blend Cool Whip into Jello until smooth. Fold in strawberries. Chill until mixture will mound. Spoon into graham cracker crust. Refrigerate at least 2 hours before serving.

Mandarin Cake

See Frosting Below

1) 1 package yellow cake mix
2) 4 eggs
3) 1 (11 ounce) can mandarin oranges (reserve liquid)
4) 3/4 cup vegetable oil

Pour 1 cup liquid from mandarin oranges into measuring cup. If there is not enough to make 1 cup, add water. Chop oranges. Mix all remaining ingredients with mandarin liquid. Pour into 3 greased pans lined with wax paper. Bake 20 to 25 minutes at 350 degrees.

Mandarin Cake Frosting

1) 1 (20 ounce) can crushed pineapple with juice
2) 1 (3 1/2 ounce) package vanilla pudding mix
3) 1 (12 ounce) carton Cool Whip

Mix all ingredients and frost cake. Refrigerate.

Cherry Pie Cake

1) 2 (21 ounce) cans cherry pie filling
2) 1/2 cup pecans
3) 1 box yellow cake mix
4) 1/2 cup margarine

Mix cake with margarine to look like crumbled pie crust. Save 1 cup for topping. Spread rest in bottom of 9x12-inch greased pan. Pour pie filling on top. Put remaining "pie crust" and pecans on top. Bake 45 minutes at 350 degrees.

Apple-Carrot Cake

See Frosting Below

1)   1 package carrot cake mix
2)   2/3 cup vegetable oil
3)   3 eggs
4)   1 cup applesauce

Combine mix, oil and eggs. Beat at medium speed for 3 minutes. Add applesauce and beat 1 minute. Pour into greased and floured tube pan. Bake 35 minutes at 350 degrees.

Apple-Carrot Glaze

1)   1 (4 ounce) package cream cheese, softened
2)   1 cup powdered sugar
3)   3 tablespoons lemon juice

Beat cream cheese until fluffy. Add sugar and lemon juice until smooth. Spread over warm cake.

Real Fruit Cake

1)   1 1/2 pounds mixed candied fruit
2)   1 (3 1/2 ounce) can coconut
3)   1 pound pecan pieces
4)   1 (14 ounce) can sweetened condensed milk

Mix all ingredients and spread in greased 5x9-inch loaf pan. Bake 2 hours at 250 degrees.

Flop Cake

See Frosting Below

1) 2 cups flour
2) 2 teaspoons baking soda
3) 1 1/2 cups sugar
4) 1 (20 ounce) can crushed pineapple

Combine flour, soda and sugar. Add pineapple and mix well. Pour into greased and floured 9x13-inch pan. Bake 20 to 30 minutes at 350 degrees.

Flop Cake Frosting

1) 1 (14 ounce) can sweetened condensed milk
2) 1/2 cup margarine, melted
3) 1/2 teaspoon vanilla
4) 1 cup flaked coconut

Combine milk and margarine and bring to a boil. Stirring constantly, boil for 4 minutes. Add coconut and mix. Spread over cake while it is hot.

Chocolate Pound Cake

1) 1 package chocolate cake mix
2) 1/2 cup oil
3) 1 1/4 cups water
4) 4 eggs

Blend all ingredients and beat medium speed for 2 minutes. Pour into greased and floured tube pan. Bake 1 hour at 350 degrees.

Lemon Cake

See Frosting Below

1)   1 package lemon with pudding cake mix
2)   4 eggs
3)   2/3 cup vegetable oil
4)   1 cup lemon-lime soda

Combine eggs with cake mix, one egg at a time. Add oil and beat for 3 minutes at medium speed. Add lemon-lime soda and beat 1 minute. Pour into a greased and floured 9x13-inch pan. Bake 30 minutes at 350 degrees.

Lemon Cake Glaze

1)   1/2 cup margarine, melted
2)   2 cups powdered sugar
3)   6 to 7 tablespoons lemon-lime soda
4)   1/2 teaspoon lemon extract

Combine and spread over warm cake.

Time Saving Idea: When you are in the mood to bake, prepare two cakes, one to serve now and one to freeze for later. Allow the cake for the freezer to cool. Pack in plastic freezer bags either whole or sliced. Freeze for up to six months. We prefer to frost our cakes the day we plan on serving them.

Fruit Cocktail Cake

See Frosting Below

1) 4 cups flour
2) 2 cups sugar
3) 2 teaspoons baking soda
4) 1 (30 ounce) can fruit cocktail, undrained

Mix all ingredients with a spoon. Pour into a 9x13-inch greased and floured pan. Bake 45 minutes at 300 degrees.

Fruit Cocktail Cake Frosting

1) 1 cup sugar
2) 1 (12 ounce) can evaporated milk
3) 1/2 cup butter
4) 1 teaspoon vanilla

Cook all ingredients over medium heat until thick. Spread over warm cake.

*Preparation Idea: Save the wrappers from margarine or
butter in a ziplock bag in the refrigerator.
When a recipe calls for a greased pan,
use the wrappers to grease the pan.*

Strawberry Cake

See Frosting Below

1) 1 package strawberry cake mix
2) 3/4 cup water
3) 3 eggs
4) 1 (8 1/4 ounce) can crushed pineapple (save 1/4 cup liquid)

Mix all ingredients including 1/4 cup reserved liquid. Pour into a 9x13-inch greased and floured pan. Bake 45 to 55 minutes at 350 degrees.

Strawberry Cake Frosting

1) 1 (3 1/2 ounce) package vanilla instant pudding mix
2) 1 cup milk
3) 1 cup whipping cream

Mix pudding and milk. Set aside. Beat whipping cream with flavoring until stiff. Fold pudding mixture and whipped cream mixture together. Frost cake. Refrigerate.

Occasionally check your oven for temperature accuracy.
We recommend investing in a good oven thermometer.

Chocolate Chip Cookies

1) 1 package yellow cake mix
2) 1/2 cup oil
3) 2 eggs
4) 1 (6 ounce) package semi-sweet chocolate chips

Mix all ingredients. Drop by teaspoonful on lightly greased cookie sheet. Bake 10 minutes at 375 degrees.

Coconut Chocolate Cookies

1) 1 package chocolate cake mix
2) 1 cup flaked coconut
3) 2 eggs
4) 1/2 cup oil

Mix all ingredients. Place mixture in a greased and floured 15x10x1-inch pan. Bake 15 to 20 minutes at 350 degrees. Cool and cut into bars.

Quick Cookies

1) 1/4 cup brown sugar
2) 1/2 cup margarine, softened
3) 1 cup flour
4) 1 teaspoon vanilla

Mix all ingredients and form into 1-inch balls. Place on cookie sheet and bake 10 minutes at 350 degrees.

Praline Shortbread Cookies

1) 1 cup butter, softened
2) 3/4 cup packed brown sugar
3) 1 1/2 cups flour
4) 1/2 cup ground pecans

Cream butter and add sugar. Beat at medium speed until light and fluffy. Stir in flour and pecans...dough will be stiff. Press onto bottom of greased and floured 15x10x1-inch pan. Score into 2-inch squares. Bake 20 minutes at 325 degrees. Break into wedges.

Shortbread Cookies

1) 1 cup butter, softened
2) 3/4 cup powdered sugar
3) 1/4 cup cornstarch
4) 1 3/4 cups flour

Cream butter; gradually add powdered sugar and cornstarch. Beat until light and fluffy. Add flour. Press into lightly greased and floured 15x10x1-inch pan. Bake 30 to 35 minutes at 325 degrees.

Shortbread

1) 1 cup butter, softened
2) 1/2 cup powdered sugar, sifted
3) 2 cups flour
4) Sugar

Cream butter. Add powdered sugar, beating until light and fluffy. Stir in flour...mixture will be stiff. Press onto bottom of greased and floured 15x10x1-inch pan. Prick all over with fork. Chill 30 minutes. Bake 5 minutes at 375 degrees. Reduce heat to 300 degrees and bake 25 minutes or until golden brown. Cut into 1 1/2-inch squares while warm. Sprinkle with sugar.

Praline Graham Cookies

1) 1 package graham crackers
2) 1 cup butter
3) 1 1/2 cups brown sugar
4) 2 cups pecans, chopped

Put crackers in single layer on 15x10x1-inch pan. Boil margarine, sugar and pecans for 2 minutes, stirring constantly. Spread on graham crackers. Bake 10 minutes at 350 degrees.

Walnut-Spice Cookies

1) 1/4 cup sugar
2) 1 teaspoon pumpkin pie spice seasoning
3) 1 egg white, room temperature
4) 1 cup walnuts, finely chopped

Mix sugar and seasoning. Beat egg white on high for 1 minute. Gradually add sugar mixture. Beat until stiff. Fold in walnuts. Drop onto greased cookie sheet. Bake 35 to 40 minutes at 250 degrees.

Sweet Cereal Puffs

1) 3 egg whites
2) 2/3 cup sugar
3) 4 cups Total cereal
4) 1/4 teaspoon vanilla (optional)

Beat egg whites to a foam. Add sugar gradually, beating until stiff. Add vanilla if desired. Fold in cereal. Drop 2-inches apart on greased cookie sheet. Bake 14 minutes or until brown at 325 degrees. Cool.

Peanut Butter Cookies I

No Bake

1) 1 cup sugar
2) 1 cup corn syrup
3) 1 (12 ounce) jar crunchy peanut butter
4) 5 cups crisp rice cereal

Melt sugar and corn syrup. Add peanut butter, cereal; mix. Form into 1-inch balls. Place on wax paper. Cool.

Peanut Butter Cookies II

1) 1 cup crunchy peanut butter
2) 1 egg
3) 1 cup sugar
4) 1 teaspoon vanilla

Mix all ingredients and form into 1-inch balls. Press flat on greased cookie sheet with a fork. Bake 10 minutes at 350 degrees.

Easy Peanut Butter Cookies

1) 1 (14 ounce) can sweetened condensed milk
2) 3/4 cup peanut butter
3) 2 cups biscuit mix
4) 1 teaspoon vanilla extract

Beat milk and peanut butter until smooth. Add biscuit mix and vanilla and mix well. Shape into 1-inch balls. Place 2 inches apart on ungreased baking sheet. Flatten with fork. Bake 6 to 8 minutes at 375 degrees.

Peanut Butter Fudge

1)   1 cup peanut butter
2)   1 cup corn syrup
3)   1 1/4 cups non-fat dry milk
4)   1 1/4 cups confectioners sugar

Mix all ingredients and stir until well blended. Knead. Form into balls and roll in confectioners sugar.

Chocolate Chip Candy

1)   1 (18 ounce) package chocolate chips
2)   1 cup chopped nuts
3)   1 1/2 teaspoon vanilla
4)   1 (14 ounce) can sweetened condensed milk

Melt chips over low heat with sweetened condensed milk. Remove from heat and stir in nuts and vanilla. Spread onto wax paper lined 8x8-inch pan. Chill 2 hours or until firm. Cut into squares.

Good Candy

1)   1 (12 ounce) package chocolate chips
2)   1 (12 ounce) package butterscotch chips
3)   2 tablespoons peanut butter
4)   2 cups chopped pecans

Melt chips in double boiler. Add peanut butter. Stir. Add pecans. Mix well. Drop by teaspoonful on waxed paper. Cool.

Party Mints

1) 1 (8 ounce) package cream cheese, softened
2) 2 (16 ounce) boxes powdered sugar
3) 1 teaspoon peppermint flavoring
4) Food coloring (your choice)

Gradually add cream cheese to sugar. Add food coloring and peppermint. The mixture will be very stiff. Form into balls and place on waxed paper. Flatten each ball with bottom of a glass. Dust with sugar if desired.

Peanut Butter Cups

1) 1 (16 ounce) box powdered sugar, sifted
2) 1 quart peanut butter
3) 1 pound margarine
4) 1 (12 ounce) package milk chocolate chips

Cream margarine and peanut butter. Add sugar. Knead with fingers. Put into a 9x13-inch pan. Melt chocolate chips in double boiler and pour over peanut butter mixture. Refrigerate until firm. Cut into squares.

Tumbleweeds

1)   1 (12 ounce) package butterscotch chips
2)   2 tablespoons peanut butter
3)   1 (12 ounce) can peanuts
4)   1 (4 ounce) can shoestring potatoes

Melt chips and peanut butter in double boiler. Combine peanuts and shoestring potatoes to butterscotch mixture. Drop by teaspoonful onto waxed paper. Cool.

MORE
OF THE
FOUR
INGREDIENT
COOKBOOK

By Linda Coffee and Emily Cale

Published by Coffee and Cale

Acknowledgements

We really want to acknowledge Phil Houseal who made working on the computer look so easy! And a special thanks to all of you who so kindly purchased our first cookbook, *The Four Ingredient Cookbook,* reordered more for friends and family, and shared your recipes with us for this cookbook!

Special Edition   Volumes I, II, III
1998   30,000 copies

4 Ingredient Cookbook
More 4 Ingredient Cookbook
Low-Fat & Light 4 Ingredient Cookbook
1994-1998   300,000 copies

Copyright © 1994
Linda Coffee and Emily Cale
Kerrville, Texas

MANUFACTURED IN THE USA BY

cookbook
resources

541 Doubletree Drive
Highland Village, Texas 75067
(972) 317-0245

to busy people everywhere...

We're still cooking!

With the startling success of our first cookbook, *The Four Ingredient Cookbook,* we realized that we were not alone! We were not the only ones that had hectic lives, leaving us too tired or too busy to cook. We've received hundreds of letters thanking us for writing a non-nonsense type of cookbook and asking for more.

So, thanks to the many of you that have shared your little recipes, we now have our second cookbook — *More of the Four Ingredient Cookbook.* We hope you will continue to enjoy these simple, concise and easy to follow recipes.

Thank you for all your support!

Happy "little" cooking,
Linda Coffee and Emily Cale

Table of Contents

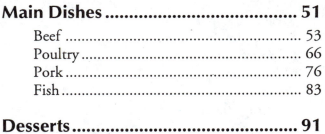

Standard Equipment
Used in *The Four Ingredient Cookbook*

Baking Sheet — 15"x10"x1"
Basting Brush
Blender
Cake Pans —
5"x9" loaf, 9"x13" sheet, tube cake pans
Can Opener
Covered Casseroles
Cookie Sheets
Colander
Cutting Board
Double Boiler
Draining Spoon
Electric Mixer
Grater
Knives and Knife Sharpener
Measuring Cups — liquid (glass) and dry
Measuring Spoons
Mixing Bowls — assorted
Mixing Spoons and Wooden Spoons
Muffin Pan
Pie Pan — 9"
Roasting Pan, Rack, Lid
Rolling Pin
Saucepans with Covers
Skillets with Covers
Spatula
Vegetable Peeler
Whisk

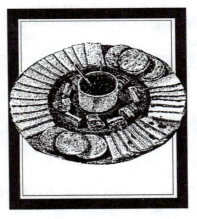

Appetizers

Artichoke Ranch Dip

1) 1 (8 1/2 ounce) can artichoke hearts, drained and finely chopped
2) 1 tablespoon ranch salad dressing mix
3) 1 (8 ounce) package cream cheese, softened
4) 1 cup mayonnaise

Mix above ingredients and refrigerate. Serve with crackers.

Mexican Avocado Dip

1) 3 large ripe avocados, mashed
2) 1 cup sour cream
3) 1 package Good Season Mexican salad dressing mix
4) 1 tablespoon lemon juice

Mix above ingredients or process in food processor until smooth. Serve with tortilla chips.

Bean and Cheese Dip

1) 1 (6 ounce) carton garlic and herbs soft spreadable cheese
2) 1 can bean with bacon soup
3) 1 cup sour cream
4) 1/2 teaspoon onion powder

In saucepan, melt cheese with soup. Add sour cream and onion. Heat for 5 minutes on low heat. Serve with tortilla chips.

Bleu Vegetable Dip

1) 1 1/2 cups buttermilk
2) 2 cups mayonnaise
3) 1/4 cup crumbled bleu cheese
4) 1/2 package Italian salad dressing mix

Mix above ingredients and serve with assorted fresh vegetables

Curry Dip

1) 1 cup sour cream
2) 1/2 teaspoon curry powder
3) 1/4 teaspoon salt
4) Fresh shrimp (cooked, peeled and cleaned)

Mix sour cream, curry powder and salt. Serve with fresh shrimp.

Salsa Cheese Dip

1) 1 cup picante sauce or salsa
2) 1 pound Velveeta cheese, cubed
3) 2 tablespoons chopped cilantro
4) Chips

Melt cheese and salsa over low heat in saucepan until cheese is melted. Stir in cilantro. Serve hot with tortilla chips.

Shrimp Dip

1) 1 (8 ounce) carton sour cream
2) 1 (8 ounce) package cream cheese, softened
3) 1 package Italian salad dressing mix
4) 1 (4 1/4 ounce) can shrimp, drained and finely chopped

Mix above ingredients and chill. Serve with crackers.

Veggie Dippin' Dip

1) 1 (8 ounce) package cream cheese, softened
2) 2 tablespoons milk
3) 1 teaspoon prepared horseradish
4) 1/2 cup parsley

Mix above ingredients and beat until smooth. Serve with raw vegetables.

Almond Delight Dip

1) 2 (8 ounce) cartons vanilla low fat yogurt
2) 1/8 teaspoon almond extract
3) 2 tablespoons chopped toasted almonds
4) Apple slices

Combine yogurt and almond extract. Chill at least 1 hour. Sprinkle with chopped almonds. Serve with apple slices. (To prevent apple slices from darkening, toss with lemon juice.)

Bleu Cheese Walnut Dip

1)   4 ounces cream cheese, softened
2)   1/4 cup crumbled bleu cheese
3)   1 (12 ounce) carton cottage cheese
4)   2 tablespoons walnuts, finely chopped

Blend first three ingredients until smooth. Stir in walnuts. Serve with fresh fruit.

Caramel Fruit Dip

1)   1 (8 ounce) package cream cheese, softened
2)   1/2 cup brown sugar
3)   1 teaspoon vanilla
4)   1 cup sour cream

Mix above ingredients and chill. Serve with assorted fresh fruit.

Peppered Cheese Ball

1)   1 (8 ounce) package cream cheese, softened
2)   1 tablespoon sour cream
3)   1 teaspoon garlic powder
4)   3 tablespoons cracked peppercorns (retain 1 tablespoon for garnish)

Beat first 3 ingredients. Add 2 tablespoons cracked peppercorns and beat until fluffy. Shape into ball. Garnish with remaining 1 tablespoon peppercorn. Refrigerate. Serve with crackers.

Potato Chip Cheese Appetizers

1) 1/2 cup ranch flavored potato chips, finely crushed
2) 1 (8 ounce) package cream cheese, softened
3) 1/2 cup grated raw carrot
4) Chopped parsley

Mix first 3 ingredients and shape into tiny bite-sized balls. Roll in parsley and refrigerate until ready to serve.

Deviled Ham Log

1) 2 (4 1/2 ounce) cans deviled ham
2) 3 tablespoons pimiento stuffed green olives, chopped
3) 1 tablespoon prepared mustard
4) 1 (8 ounce) package cream cheese, softened

Mix above ingredients. Form into log and chill. Serve with crackers.

Smoked Oyster Loaf

1) 1 (3 3/4 ounce) can smoked oysters, drained and chopped
2) 1 (8 ounce) package cream cheese, softened
3) 2 tablespoons Worcestershire sauce
4) 2 tablespoons Lipton onion soup mix

Mix above ingredients and shape into loaf. Refrigerate. Serve with crackers.

Cocktail Sausage Balls

1) 1 pound hot bulk sausage
2) 3 cups biscuit mix
3) 1 (8 ounce) jar Cheez Whiz
4) 1/4 teaspoon garlic powder (optional)

Mix above ingredients and shape into cocktail-sized meatballs. Place on baking pan and bake for 25 minutes or until lightly browned at 300 degrees.

Wheat Cheese Snacks

1) 1 cup margarine
2) 2 (8 ounce) cups shredded American cheese
3) 8 to 10 cups (17.2 ounce box) spoon-size shredded wheat
4) 1 tablespoon Cajun seasoning

Melt margarine and cheese over low heat. In a large bowl, pour cheese mixture over shredded wheat and Cajun seasoning. Toss to coat. Spread on cookie sheet to cool. Store in airtight container. If snacks become soft, re-crisp them by placing on baking sheet in a 250 degree oven for 45 to 60 minutes, stirring occasionally.

To keep cut fruits from discoloring, sprinkle lemon or pineapple juice over them.

Mini Quiches

1)   1 can refrigerator butterflake biscuits
2)   1 cup shredded Monterey Jack with pepper cheese
3)   2 eggs
4)   2 green onions with tops, finely chopped

Separate rolls and divide each roll into three sections. Press dough section in lightly greased mini-muffin cups stretching slightly to form shell. Mix cheese, eggs and onions and spoon mixture into shells. Bake for 15 minutes or until firm at 375 degrees.

Tortilla Roll-ups

1)   1 (8 ounce) package cream cheese, softened
2)   1 teaspoon taco seasoning
3)   1/3 cup picante sauce
4)   12 flour tortillas

Beat cream cheese until smooth. Add taco seasoning, picante sauce and mix well. Spread mixture on each tortilla. Roll tortilla tightly. Place seam side down in airtight container. Chill at least 2 hours. Slice each roll into 1-inch slices forming a pinwheel. Arrange on plate to serve.

Monterey Cheese Crisps

1) 1 pound Monterey Jack cheese, sliced 1/4-inch thick
2) Cayenne pepper
3) 1/4 teaspoon garlic powder (optional)
4) Sprinkle paprika (optional)

Cut cheese into 1/4-inch thick slices. Place slices 3 inches apart on a non-stick baking sheet — cheese will spread while baking. Sprinkle with cayenne pepper, garlic powder and paprika if desired. Bake for 10 minutes or until golden brown at 400 degrees, watch closely. Remove crisps and cool on paper towels. Stores well in airtight container.

Cheese Chile Appetizer

1) 2 (8 ounce) packages cream cheese, softened
2) 2 large eggs, slightly beaten
3) 2 1/2 cups shredded Monterey Jack cheese
4) 1 (4 ounce) can chopped green chilies

Combine above ingredients and spread into lightly greased pan. Bake for 30 minutes at 325 degrees. Cut into squares. Serve with tortilla chips.

Crab Delight

1) 2 (8 ounce) packages cream cheese, softened
2) 1 (8 ounce) package imitation crab flakes
3) 2 tablespoons finely chopped green onions
4) 1/2 cup bottled horseradish sauce

Beat cream cheese until smooth and blend in remaining ingredients. Spread into pie plate. Bake uncovered for 20 minutes at 375 degrees. Serve with crackers or vegetables.

Nippy Shrimp

1)   1/2 teaspoon garlic
2)   1/2 cup chili sauce
3)   30 small shrimp, cooked and peeled
4)   10 slices bacon, cut into thirds

Combine garlic and chili sauce. Pour over shrimp. Cover and refrigerate several hours or overnight, stirring occasionally. Fry bacon until partially cooked, but still limp. Drain. Wrap each marinated shrimp in a bacon piece. Secure with a wooden toothpick. Broil 2 to 3 inches from heat until bacon is crisp.

Ham Crescent Snacks

1)   1 can refrigerator crescent rolls
2)   4 thin slices ham
3)   4 teaspoons prepared mustard
4)   1 cup shredded Swiss cheese

Unroll dough into 4 long rectangles. Press perforations to seal. Place ham slices on rectangles. Spread ham with mustard and sprinkle with cheese. Starting at longest side, roll up in jelly roll fashion. Cut into 1/2-inch slices. Place cut side down on ungreased cookie sheet. Bake for 15 to 20 minutes or until lightly browned at 375 degrees.

Dill Croutons

1) 1 (24 ounce) package oyster crackers
2) 3/4 cup vegetable oil
3) 2 tablespoons dill weed
4) 1 (2 ounce) package ranch dressing mix

Combine oil, dill weed and dressing mix until well blended. Add crackers and blend until all oil is absorbed. Store in airtight container.

Salami Roll-ups

1) 1 (8 ounce) package cream cheese, softened
2) 1 teaspoon prepared horseradish
3) 12 ounces salami, thinly sliced
4) 1/2 teaspoon seasoning salt (optional)

Combine cream cheese and horseradish with seasoning salt if desired. Spread 1 1/2 teaspoons of mixture on each salami slice. Roll up and secure with toothpicks. Makes 36 appetizers.

Tortellini Appetizer

1) 1 (9 ounce) package meat filled tortellini, cooked and drained
2) 1 tablespoon soy sauce
3) 1 tablespoon olive oil
4) 1 tablespoon sesame seed

Combine soy sauce, oil and sesame seed. Pour over tortellini and toss to coat. Cover and refrigerate up to 24 hours. Preheat oven to 425 degrees. Spread tortellini on foil lined baking sheet sprayed with Pam. Bake 15 to 18 minutes or until edges are golden.

Spicy Pecans

1)   1 tablespoon butter
2)   1/2 to 1 teaspoon Cajun seasoning, to taste
3)   1/2 teaspoon Worcestershire sauce
4)   1 cup pecan halves

In oven proof skillet (cast iron works well) over medium heat, melt butter. Add Worcestershire sauce and Cajun seasoning. Add pecans and stir until well coated. Place skillet in 225 degree oven and bake for 45 minutes or until pecans are crisp.

Artichoke Appetizer

1)   1 (8 1/2 ounce) can artichoke hearts, drained and chopped
2)   6 eggs
3)   1 cup grated Jack cheese with jalapenos
4)   12 saltine crackers, crushed

Mix all ingredients and pour into 9x9-inch pan. Bake for 45 minutes at 350 degrees. Cut into squares. Serve hot or cold.

Crab Appetizers

1)   1/2 pound Velveeta cheese
2)   1/4 cup margarine
3)   1 (6 ounce) can crab meat
4)   1 package garlic flavored Melba toast

Melt cheese and margarine. Remove from heat. Add crab meat and mix. Spoon onto Melba toast and broil until slightly browned.

Ham and Pimiento Spread

1)   1 1/2 cups finely chopped cooked ham
2)   1 (4 ounce) jar pimiento, drained and chopped
3)   1/2 cup fresh parsley, chopped
4)   1/2 cup mayonnaise

Mix all ingredients and stir well. Chill. Serve on party rye bread or with crackers.

Smokey Spread

1)   8 ounces shredded cheddar cheese
2)   1 (8 ounce) package cream cheese, softened
3)   4 bacon strips, cooked and crumbled
4)   1 tablespoon Worcestershire sauce

Combine cheddar cheese and cream cheese. Mix until well blended. Add remaining ingredients. Mix well and chill. Serve with crackers.

Beer Bread

1)   3 cups self-rising flour
2)   3 tablespoons sugar
3)   1 (12 ounce) can beer
4)   Melted butter (optional)

Combine first 3 ingredients and pour into a greased loaf pan. Bake at 350 degrees for 45 minutes or until golden brown. Brush with melted butter if desired.

Twist Sticks

1) 1/2 cup sour cream
2) 1/2 package savory herb with garlic soup mix
3) 1 (8 ounce) package refrigerator crescent rolls
4) I Can't Believe It's Butter spray (optional)

Combine sour cream and soup mix. Spread out crescent rolls into one long piece of dough, pressing seams together. Spread mixture evenly onto dough. Cut dough into 1-inch strips and twist each strip loosely. Bake on ungreased (or lightly sprayed) cookie sheet for 12 to 15 minutes at 375 degrees.

7-Up Biscuits

1) 1/4 cup 7-Up
2) 1/4 cup buttermilk
3) 2 cups biscuit mix
4) 2 tablespoons butter, melted

Mix first three ingredients and knead until smooth and elastic. Place on floured board and spread dough gently until 1-inch thick. Cut into biscuits and place on greased 9-inch baking pan. Brush tops with melted butter. Bake 20 minutes at 450 degrees. Cool slightly before serving.

Yammy Biscuits

1) 2 3/4 cups biscuit mix (retain 1/4 cup to flour board)
2) 1 (17 ounce) can yams in syrup, undrained and mashed
3) 1/4 cup butter, melted
4) Pinch cinnamon

Place biscuit mix in large bowl and cut yams and butter into it. Add a pinch of cinnamon if desired. Mix well. Knead on floured board until dough is not sticky. (Knead in additional biscuit mix, if necessary.) Pat out to 1/2-inch thickness and cut into biscuits. Bake 12 to 15 minutes at 400 degrees.

If you're a chile pepper lover, an easy appetizer is to cut them in half lengthwise and fill them with tuna, chicken or egg salad or all three.

Salads

Lime Coke Salad

1) 1 (6 ounce) package lime Jello plus 1 cup boiling water
2) 1 cup regular Coke
3) 1 (10 ounce) medium bottle maraschino cherries, drained and chopped
4) 1 cup pecans, chopped

Dissolve Jello in hot water. Add Coke, cherries and pecans. Place in serving dish. Refrigerate until firm.

Fruit Cocktail Salad

1) 1 (17 ounce) can fruit cocktail, with syrup
2) 1 (3 ounce) package strawberry Jello
3) 1 (3 ounce) package cream cheese, softened
4) 1 (8 ounce) carton Cool Whip

Heat fruit cocktail with juice and Jello to boiling point. Remove from heat. Add cream cheese and stir until it melts. Fold in Cool Whip. Place in serving container and refrigerate.

Ice Cream Salad

1) 1 (3 ounce) package orange Jello plus 1 cup boiling water
2) 1 pint vanilla ice cream, softened
3) 1/2 cup pecans, chopped
4) 1 (8 ounce) can crushed pineapple, drained

Dissolve Jello in boiling water. Mix in remaining ingredients and place in serving dish. Refrigerate until set.

Mango Salad

1) 2 (3 ounce) packages lemon Jello
2) 2 cups boiling water
3) 1 (26 ounce) jar mango with juice, mashed
4) 1 (8 ounce) package cream cheese, softened

Dissolve Jello in boiling water. Mix mangos, juice and cream cheese together. Combine with Jello mixture. Place in serving dish. Refrigerate until set.

Orange Salad

1) 1 (8 ounce) can crushed pineapple, drained
2) 1 (3 ounce) package orange Jello
3) 1 (12 ounce) carton small curd cottage cheese
4) 1 (8 ounce) carton Cool Whip

Mix pineapple, orange Jello and cottage cheese. Fold in Cool Whip and chill until ready to serve.

Frozen Cranberry Salad

1) 1 (16 ounce) whole cranberry sauce
2) 1 (8 ounce) can crushed pineapple, drained
3) 1 banana, mashed
4) 1 (12 ounce) carton Cool Whip

Mix above ingredients. Place in serving container and freeze.

Sliced Frozen Fruit Salad

1) 1 (17 ounce) chunky mixed fruits
2) Lettuce
3) Cool Whip or Whipped Cream
4) 4 maraschino cherries (optional)

Freeze fruit cocktail in the can. Remove from freezer and open both ends of can. Push frozen fruit cocktail through can and cut into 4 slices. Place on a lettuce bed and top with Cool Whip or whipped cream. Add a maraschino cherry on top if desired.

Layered Fruit Salad

1) 3 cups orange sections
2) 1 (15 1/4 ounce) can crushed pineapple, drained
3) 1/2 cup flaked coconut
4) 3 tablespoons honey

Layer 1 1/2 cups oranges, 1/2 pineapple, 1/4 cup coconut. Repeat layer. Drizzle with honey and cover. Chill overnight.

Waldorf Salad

1) 4 cups apples, chopped
2) 3/4 cup raisins
3) 1/2 cup pecan pieces
4) 1/2 cup mayonnaise

Combine ingredients. Refrigerate until ready to serve.

Mandarin Salad

Orange Juice Dressing follows

1)   2 tomatoes, peeled and sliced
2)   2 (11 ounce) cans mandarin oranges, drained
3)   1/2 cup onion, thinly sliced
4)   3 cups lettuce leaves, torn into bite-size pieces

Combine ingredients. Good served with orange juice dressing.
(Recipe follows.)

Orange Juice Dressing

1)   1/4 cup orange juice
2)   2 teaspoons red wine vinegar
3)   1 tablespoon vegetable oil
4)   2 teaspoons honey

Mix above ingredients and pour over mandarin salad.

Frozen Pineapple Cranberry Salad

1)   1 (20 ounce) can crushed pineapple, drained
2)   1 (16 ounce) can whole cranberry sauce
3)   1 cup sour cream
4)   1/2 cup pecans, chopped

Combine all ingredients and place in a 8x8-inch pan. Freeze. Cut
into squares before serving.

Avocado Grapefruit Salad

1) 1 (26 ounce) jar grapefruit sections, drained
2) 2 ripe avocados, peeled and sliced
3) 1/2 cup red onion, thinly sliced
4) Prepared poppy seed dressing

Combine grapefruit, avocados and onions. Serve with dressing on a bed of lettuce.

Nutty Banana Salad

1) 2/3 cup mayonnaise
2) 2 tablespoons sugar
3) 6 medium bananas
4) 1 1/3 cups peanuts, finely chopped

Add sugar to mayonnaise and mix well. Roll the bananas in mayonnaise mixture. Roll the bananas in the nuts. Slice and serve on a crisp bed of lettuce.

Cole Slaw

1) 1 head cabbage, shredded
2) 1 (4 ounce) jar pimiento, chopped (retain fluid)
3) 1 (12 ounce) can peanuts
4) 1 cup mayonnaise

Blend mayonnaise with the fluid from the pimientos. Combine all ingredients and chill.

Marinated Asparagus Salad

1)   1 (15 ounce) can asparagus pieces, drained
2)   1 (8 1/2 ounce) can small early peas, drained
3)   3 hard boiled eggs, chopped
4)   1 package garlic salad dressing mix, prepared

Combine asparagus, peas and eggs. Pour dressing over mixture and stir gently. Cover and chill several hours. Drain and serve on a lettuce bed.

Corn Salad

1)   2 (16 ounce) cans Mexicorn, drained
2)   1 green pepper, chopped
3)   1 onion, chopped
4)   1 cup Catalina salad dressing

Combine ingredients. Chill several hours. Serve cold.

Cucumber Salad

1)   4 large cucumbers, peeled and sliced
2)   2 onions, sliced
3)   1/2 teaspoon sugar
4)   1 cup sour cream

Place cucumbers and onions in bowl. Sprinkle with sugar. Add sour cream and mix. Salt and pepper to taste. Refrigerate for several hours.

Pea Salad

1) 1 (10 ounce) package frozen green peas, thawed
2) 1/2 cup cheddar cheese, cubed
3) 1/2 cup celery, chopped
4) 1/2 cup sour cream

Combine above ingredients. Salt and pepper to taste. Refrigerate for several hours. Serve on bed of lettuce.

Spinach Salad

1) 1 pound spinach, torn into bite-size pieces
2) 1 medium red onion, thinly sliced
3) 1 (11 ounce) can mandarin oranges, drained
4) 1/2 cup almonds, toasted

Combine ingredients. Good served with poppy seed dressing.

Sunny Spinach Salad

1) 1 pound spinach, torn into bite-size pieces
2) 1 medium red onion, thinly sliced
3) 1 (6 ounce) package dried apricots, chopped
4) 1/3 cup toasted salted sunflower seeds

Combine ingredients. Good served with vinaigrette dressing.

Super Spinach Salad

1) 1 pound spinach, torn into bite-size pieces
2) 8 ounces fresh mushrooms, sliced
3) 8 slices bacon, fried and crumbled
4) Italian or ranch dressing

Place spinach, mushrooms and crumbled bacon in salad bowl. Serve with Italian or ranch salad dressing.

Green Bean Salad

1) 1 (16 ounce) can French style green beans, drained
2) 8 cherry tomatoes, halved
3) 4 fresh green onions, sliced
4) 1/2 cup French dressing

Combine ingredients. Chill at least 1 hour before serving. Serve on a crisp bed of lettuce.

Carrot Salad

1) 2 cups grated carrots
2) 1/2 cup raisins
3) 1 (8 3/4 ounce) can pineapple tidbits, drained
4) 1/3 cup mayonnaise

Combine above ingredients and serve on a crisp bed of lettuce.

Rice Salad

1) 1/2 cup Italian salad dressing
2) 1/2 cup mayonnaise
3) 1 (10 ounce) package frozen mixed vegetables, thawed
4) 3 cups cooked rice

Blend Italian dressing and mayonnaise. Stir in vegetables and rice. Toss well. Chill until ready to serve.

Seafood Salad

1) 1 (8 ounce) package Crab Delights (flake style)
2) 1/2 cup mayonnaise
3) 2 stalks celery, chopped
4) 3 tablespoons finely chopped onion

Combine ingredients. Serve on a crisp bed of lettuce

Shrimp and Rice Salad

1) 2 cups cooked rice
2) 12 ounces shrimp, cooked and peeled
3) 1 (10 ounce) package frozen peas/pearl onions, thawed
4) 1/2 cup Italian salad dressing

Mix above ingredients and serve on a crisp bed of lettuce.

Pasta Salad

1) 1 (16 ounce) package elbow macaroni pasta, cooked, rinsed and drained
2) 1 medium sweet red pepper, cut into strips
3) 1 cup fresh mushrooms, sliced
4) 1 cup broccoli flowerets

Combine ingredients and toss well. Chill and serve with Caesar salad dressing.

Seafood Pasta Salad

1) 1 pound vegetable rotini pasta, cooked, rinsed and drained
2) 1 (6 ounce) can pitted ripe olives, drained
3) 1 (10 ounce) package frozen chopped broccoli, thawed and drained
4) 1 (8 ounce) package imitation crab flakes

Combine pasta with remaining ingredients. Toss and chill until ready to serve. Serve with Italian or ranch salad dressing.

Never put tomatoes in the refrigerator, the cold temperature stops the ripening process and kills tomato flavor.

Vegetables

Marinated Artichoke Hearts

1)   2 (9 ounce) packages frozen artichoke hearts
2)   1 Kraft House Italian with Olive Oil salad dressing
3)   1/4 cup finely chopped onion (optional)
4)   Sprinkle garlic powder

Cook artichoke hearts as directed on package. Drain well. Cool. Sprinkle with onion and garlic powder if desired. Pour salad dressing over artichokes. Toss and refrigerate overnight.

Lemon Asparagus and Baby Carrots

1)   1 pound asparagus, steamed until crisp tender
2)   1/2 pound small carrots, steamed until crisp tender
3)   Lemon pepper
4)   1 tablespoon lemon juice

Drain asparagus and carrots. In casserole, combine carrots and asparagus. Cover and refrigerate. When ready to serve, sprinkle with lemon pepper and lemon juice. Serve cold.

Asparagus in Lemon Butter

1)   1 pound asparagus, remove tough stems
2)   2 tablespoons butter, melted
3)   1/2 teaspoon grated lemon peel
4)   2 tablespoons fresh lemon juice

Cut asparagus in pieces about 1 1/2 inches long. Simmer asparagus in water. enough to cover, for about 6 minutes or until crisp-tender. Drain. In saucepan combine all ingredients. Cook over medium heat for 2 minutes. Stir and serve warm.

Asparagus with Curry Sauce

1)   2 (10 ounce) packages frozen asparagus spears
2)   1/2 cup mayonnaise
3)   2 teaspoons curry powder
4)   1 1/2 teaspoons lemon juice

Cook asparagus and drain. Combine mayonnaise, curry powder and lemon juice. Pour over asparagus. Serve warm.

Sauteed Broccoli

1)   1 (10 ounce) package frozen broccoli
2)   1 (10 ounce) package frozen whole kernel corn
3)   1 (4 ounce) can sliced mushrooms, drained
4)   1/2 cup margarine

Melt margarine in large skillet. Saute broccoli, corn and mushrooms in melted margarine until crisp-tender. Serve warm. Season to taste.

Italian Style Broccoli

1)   1 1/2 pounds broccoli, cut into flowerets
2)   1/4 cup olive oil
3)   2 cloves garlic, minced
4)   2 tablespoons lemon juice

Steam broccoli in large skillet for 5 minutes until crispy tender. Remove broccoli and drain. Pour oil into skillet and add garlic. Cook over medium heat stirring constantly until garlic is lightly browned. Add broccoli and lemon juice. Toss gently. Cover and cook for an additional minute.

Brussels Sprouts

1) 2 (10 ounce) packages frozen brussels sprouts, cooked and drained
2) 4 tablespoons margarine
3) 1/3 cup soft bread crumbs
4) 4 teaspoons lemon juice

In a small skillet, saute bread crumbs and 1 tablespoon margarine. Remove bread crumbs. Add remaining 3 tablespoons margarine and lemon juice to skillet. Stir until margarine is melted. Add sprouts, toss until evenly coated and thoroughly heated. Place in serving dish. Sprinkle with bread crumbs and serve.

Dill Carrots

1) 1 pound carrots, peeled and sliced
2) 1/2 cup Italian dressing
3) 1/2 cup Green Goddess dressing
4) 1 tablespoon dillweed

Cook carrots until crispy tender and drain. Mix Italian dressing, Green Goddess dressing and dillweed together. Pour dressing mixture over carrots. Refrigerate overnight. Serve cold.

To restore sweetness in old vegetables, add a little sugar to water while cooking.

Cheesy Cauliflower

1)   1 (16 ounce) bag frozen cauliflower, cooked and drained
2)   1 can cream of chicken soup
3)   1/4 cup milk
4)   1 cup Swiss cheese, shredded

Place cauliflower in baking dish. Combine soup, milk and cheese and spread over cauliflower. Bake for 10 minutes at 350 degrees.

Scalloped Corn

1)   2 eggs, slightly beaten
2)   1 cup milk
3)   1 cup cracker crumbs
4)   2 (16 ounce) cans whole corn, drained

Blend all ingredients together. Bake in lightly greased loaf pan for 1 hour at 325 degrees.

Corn Relish

1)   2 (11 ounce) cans Mexican-style corn
2)   1/3 cup sugar
3)   1/3 cup cider vinegar
4)   1/3 cup sweet pickle relish

Combine above ingredients and bring to a boil. Simmer for 5 minutes. Remove from heat, cover and refrigerate.

Fettucine Alfredo

1) 1 (8 ounce) package fettucini, cooked and drained
2) 6 tablespoons margarine
3) 1/2 cup grated Parmesan cheese
4) 2 tablespoons half and half

In saucepan over low heat, melt margarine. Add half and half and cheese. Heat thoroughly and pour over fettucine and toss. Serve warm.

Green Bean Casserole

1) 2 (16 ounce) cans whole green beans, drained
2) 1/2 cup French dressing
3) 1/2 cup chopped onion
4) 6 to 9 strips bacon, cooked and crumbled

Combine first 3 ingredients. Place in casserole. Sprinkle with bacon and bake for 30 minutes at 350 degrees.

Green Chile Casserole

1) 1 (4 ounce) can green chilies, chopped
2) 1 can cream of chicken soup
3) 1 (8 ounce) package Colby cheese, grated
4) 10 to 12 corn tortillas, cut into wedges

Mix soup with green chilies. Layer tortillas and cheese. Pour soup mixture over top and sprinkle with remaining cheese. Bake for 30 minutes at 350 degrees.

Marvelous Mushrooms

1) 1 pound fresh mushrooms, remove stems
2) 2 tablespoons vegetable oil
3) 2 1/2 tablespoons chopped garlic
4) 2 tablespoons soy sauce

Cut mushroom stems off. Heat oil in frying pan and add garlic. Cook garlic over medium-low heat around 4 to 6 minutes. Do not let garlic burn. Add mushrooms and cook 2 to 3 minutes. Add soy sauce; toss and serve immediately.

Stir Fried Mushrooms with Bacon

1) 4 slices bacon, cut in 1/2-inch pieces
2) 8 ounces fresh mushrooms, sliced
3) 1/4 cup cooking sherry
4) 1/4 cup finely chopped onion (optional)

Stir fry bacon until crisp. Remove bacon, reserving drippings. Add mushrooms and chopped onion if desired. Stir fry for 5 to 10 minutes. Drain off excess fat. Add wine and bacon and simmer for 3 minutes.

Poppy Seed Noodles

1) 1 (8 ounce) package wide noodles, cooked and drained
2) 1/4 cup butter, melted
3) 2 tablespoons poppy seeds
4) Pepper to taste

Toss noodles with butter and poppy seeds. Season to taste.

Okra Succotash

1) 3 cups okra, sliced
2) 1 (16 ounce) can corn
3) 1 (14 1/2 ounce) can seasoned stewed tomatoes
4) 1/2 cup onion, chopped

Rinse okra under running water. Drain. Combine ingredients in a large skillet. Cover and simmer for 15 minutes. Season to taste.

Spicy Potatoes

1) 4 large baking potatoes
2) 1/4 cup olive oil
3) 1 package onion soup mix
4) 1/4 teaspoon black pepper (optional)

Cut potatoes into bite-sized chunks. Toss potatoes in oil and onion soup mix to coat. Season with black pepper if desired. Place on baking sheet. Bake for 45 minutes at 375 degrees.

Parsley New Potatoes

1) 2 (16 ounce) cans sliced new potatoes, drained
2) 1/4 cup margarine, melted
3) 1/4 cup fresh parsley, chopped
4) Salt and pepper to taste (optional)

Place new potatoes in buttered casserole. Mix margarine and parsley and pour over potatoes. Season with salt and pepper to taste. Bake 20 minutes at 350 degrees. Season to taste.

Italian Potatoes

1) 4 medium potatoes, cut in half lengthwise
2) 1/4 cup butter
3) 1 envelope Italian salad dressing mix
4) 1/3 cup grated Parmesan cheese

Spread butter on potato halves. Sprinkle salad dressing and cheese over potatoes. Bake on greased baking sheet, cut-side down, for 45 minutes at 400 degrees.

Quick Potato Cheese Bake

1) 4 cups mashed potatoes
2) 1/2 cup Parmesan cheese
3) 2 eggs, slightly beaten
4) 1/2 cup grated cheddar cheese

Combine potatoes, Parmesan cheese and eggs. Season to taste. Place in casserole. Top with cheddar cheese and bake for 25 minutes at 350 degrees.

Scalloped Potatoes

1) 8 large potatoes, thinly sliced
2) 1 can cream of chicken soup
3) 1 can cheddar cheese soup
4) 1 can milk

Slice potatoes in 1/4-inch slices. Mix soups and milk. Layer potatoes and soup mix. Top with soup mix. Bake 45 minutes or until potatoes are tender at 350 degrees.

Country Style Potatoes

1) 2 (16 ounce) cans new potatoes, drained and sliced
2) 2 tablespoons margarine, melted
3) 1 teaspoon basil
4) 1 medium onion, chopped

Melt margarine in skillet. Add potatoes and basil. Cook until potatoes are lightly browned, stirring occasionally. Add chopped onion and cook a few minutes longer. (Onion should be hot, but still crisp.)

Potatoes au Gratin

1) 1 cup half and half
2) 1 (32 ounce) package hash brown potatoes, thawed
3) 2 tablespoons margarine
4) 1/2 cup grated cheddar cheese

Heat half and half in sauce pan. Add potatoes and margarine. Simmer slowly until thickened. Pour into lightly greased baking dish. Sprinkle with cheese. Place under broiler. Broil until brown.

Chicken Flavored
Whipped Potatoes

1) 1 cup instant mashed potatoes flakes
2) 3 cups hot water
3) 1 tablespoon chicken bouillon granules
4) 1 tablespoon margarine

Dissolve chicken bouillon and margarine in hot water. Add to potatoes and mix well. Season to taste.

New Potatoes Vinaigrette

1)   2 (16 ounce) cans new potatoes
2)   1/4 cup vinaigrette dressing
3)   1 tablespoon fresh parsley, chopped
4)   Salt to taste (optional)

Heat potatoes thoroughly. Drain. Place in bowl and toss gently with dressing. Sprinkle with parsley and serve.

Stuffed Baked Sweet Potatoes

1)   6 medium sweet potatoes
2)   2 tablespoons margarine
3)   1 (8 ounce) can crushed pineapple, drained
4)   1/2 cup pecans, chopped

Bake potatoes for 1 hour at 375 degrees. Cut a 1-inch lengthwise wedge from the top of each potato. Carefully scoop pulp from shells. Mix potato pulp, margarine and pineapple. Beat until fluffy. Stuff back into potato shell and sprinkle with pecans. Bake for 12 minutes at 375 degrees.

To keep spaghetti and macaroni from sticking,
add 1 tablespoon olive oil for flavor.

Marshmallow Topped Sweet Potatoes

1) 1 (17 ounce) can yams, drained and cut in half
2) 2 tablespoons margarine
3) 1/3 cup honey
4) 1/2 cup miniature marshmallows

Cut potatoes in half and arrange in single layer in buttered baking pan. Dot with margarine and drizzle with honey. Bake 20 minutes at 350 degrees. Remove from oven and spoon honey sauce from bottom of pan over potatoes. Sprinkle with marshmallows and return to oven long enough to lightly brown marshmallow topping.

French Onion Rice

1) 1 cup long grain white rice
2) 1/4 cup margarine
3) 1 can onion soup plus 1 can water
4) 1 (4 ounce) can chopped mushrooms

Lightly brown rice in margarine. Add soup, water and mushrooms. Cover and simmer about 25 minutes or until liquid is gone. Fluff and serve.

Onions and Herb Rice

1) 1 envelope onion soup mix plus 2 cups water
2) 2 tablespoons parsley
3) 1 1/2 teaspoons basil
4) 2 cups Minute rice

Combine first 3 ingredients with water and bring to a boil. Add rice, cover and remove from heat. Let stand for 5 to 10 minutes. Fluff and serve.

Cumin Rice

1) 3 cans chicken broth
2) 2 teaspoons cumin
3) 1 1/2 cups uncooked long grain rice
4) 1/2 cup chopped green onions

Bring broth to a boil and add cumin and rice. Cover, reduce heat and simmer for 20 minutes or until liquid is gone. Add green onions and toss.

Dirty Rice

1) 1 cup uncooked white rice
2) 1 stick margarine, melted
3) 1 can onion soup
4) 1 can beef bouillon

Mix all ingredients together. Cover and bake for 1 hour at 350 degrees.

Sauteed Spinach

1) 1 pound fresh spinach
2) 2 tablespoons olive oil
3) 2 tablespoons white wine or cooking sherry
4) 1/4 cup freshly grated Parmesan cheese

Wash and dry spinach. Cook spinach in olive oil in large skillet over high heat. Stir constantly until wilted. Add wine and cook until liquid is gone. Sprinkle with Parmesan cheese and serve.

Squash Dressing

1) 6 to 8 squash, sliced, cooked and drained
2) 2 cups crumbled Mexican corn bread, prepared
3) 1 large onion, chopped
4) 1 can nacho cheese soup

Combine ingredients. Pour into baking pan. Bake 35 to 40 minutes at 350 degrees.

Potato Chip Squash Casserole

1) 4 to 6 squash, partially cooked and sliced
2) 1 can cream of mushroom soup
3) 1 cup crushed ranch flavored potato chips
4) 1 cup grated American cheese

In greased casserole, layer squash, soup (undiluted) and crushed potato chips. Repeat layer and top with grated cheese. Bake for 30 minutes at 350 degrees or until bubbly.

Baked Squash Casserole

1) 6 to 8 medium yellow squash, grated
2) 1 large onion, grated
3) 2 tablespoons margarine, melted
4) 1 cup bread crumbs

Mix above ingredients. Season to taste. Pour into greased baking dish. Bake for 30 to 45 minutes or until brown at 350 degrees.

Fried Green Tomatoes

1) 6 large firm green tomatoes, cut into 1/4 inch slices
2) 1 cup cornmeal
3) Vegetable oil
4) Salt and pepper

Dredge tomatoes in cornmeal. Season with salt and pepper. Heat oil. Add tomatoes and fry over medium-high heat until browned. Turn once.

Stir Fry Zucchini

1) 4 cups sliced zucchini
2) 1/4 cup margarine
3) 2 tablespoons lemon pepper
4) Juice of 1 lemon

Saute zucchini and lemon pepper in margarine. Cook 10 to 15 minutes, stirring frequently. Add lemon juice. Stir and serve.

Zucchini and Walnuts

1) 3 tablespoons margarine
2) 1/2 cup walnuts, coarsely chopped
3) 4 cups zucchini, cut into 1/2 inch slices
4) 1/4 teaspoon salt

Heat 1 tablespoon margarine in skillet. Add walnuts and stir until lightly brown. Remove walnuts from skillet. Heat remaining 2 tablespoons margarine and zucchini. Saute zucchini until it begins to soften. Combine walnuts with zucchini. Season to taste.

Main Dishes

Zippy Beef Casserole

Bake 350 Degrees   **45 Minutes**

1)   1 (6.8 ounce) box Rice-a-Roni
2)   1 can nacho cheese soup plus 1 can water
3)   2 eggs
4)   1 pound ground beef, browned and drained

Combine ingredients. Place in casserole. Cover and bake for
30 minutes at 350 degrees; uncover and continue baking
10 to 15 minutes.

Coney Island Burgers

Stove Top

1)   1 pound lean ground beef
2)   1/2 cup bottled BBQ sauce
3)   4 tablespoons pickle relish
4)   4 tablespoons chopped onion

Combine ingredients and form into shape of hot dogs. Saute,
turning until brown and cooked through. Place in hot dog buns
and serve with mustard.

Meat Pita Pockets

Stove Top

1)   1 1/2 pounds ground beef, browned and drained
2)   1 can chicken gumbo soup, undiluted
3)   1/3 cup chili sauce
4)   6 pita pockets

Mix first three ingredients together and simmer for 5 to
10 minutes. Spoon filling into pita pockets. Serve.

Mexican Meat Loaf

Bake 350 Degrees   1 1/2 Hours

1)   2 pounds lean ground beef
2)   1 cup picante sauce (2/3 cup in loaf and 1/3 cup over top
        of loaf)
3)   1 cup bread crumbs
4)   2 eggs, slightly beaten

Combine above ingredients, saving 1/3 cup picante sauce for
top of meatloaf. Form into a loaf and place in greased ovenproof
pan. Top with the remaining sauce. Bake at 350 degrees for
1 1/2 hours.

Chili Meat Loaf

Bake 350 Degrees   1 1/2 Hours

1)   2 pounds lean ground beef
2)   1 (15 ounce) can chili with beans
3)   2 eggs, slightly beaten
4)   1 medium onion, chopped

Combine ingredients. Shape into loaf and place into a greased
shallow baking dish. Bake at 350 degrees for 1 1/2 hours.

Frito Meat Balls

Stove Top

1)   2 pounds lean ground beef
2)   1 cup Fritos, crushed
3)   1 egg, slightly beaten
4)   1 can cream of mushroom soup plus 1/2 can water

Mix meat, Fritos and egg together. Form into meat balls and
brown in skillet. Mix soup and water and pour over meat balls.
Simmer for 30 minutes over low heat.

Quick Meat Balls

Bake 350 Degrees   **30 Minutes**

1) 2 pounds lean ground meat
2) 1/2 pound sausage
3) 1 (6 ounce) box stove top dressing
4) 3 eggs

Mix above ingredients and shape into balls. Place on baking sheet. Bake at 350 degrees for 30 minutes.

Sour Cream Meat Balls

Stove Top
Bake 350 Degrees   **30 Minutes**

1) 1 1/2 pounds lean ground beef
2) 1 (8 ounce) carton sour cream
3) 1 teaspoon garlic powder
4) 1 teaspoon salt

Mix ground beef, garlic powder, salt and 1/2 of the sour cream together. Form into balls. Brown balls in skillet and place in baking dish. Spread remaining sour cream on meat balls and bake at 350 degrees for 30 minutes.

Spanish Hamburgers

Stove Top

1) 1 pound lean ground beef
2) 1 large onion, chopped
3) 1 can tomato soup
4) 1 teaspoon chili powder

Brown hamburger and onion. Drain off fat. Add soup and chili powder to hamburger mixture. Stir and simmer until hot. Serve over hamburger buns.

Spanish Stuffed Peppers

Bake 350 Degrees   **Stove Top 25 Minutes**

1) 3 green peppers
2) 1 pound lean ground beef, browned and drained
3) 1 (15 ounce) can Spanish rice
4) 2 tablespoons catsup

Cut green peppers in half and remove pulp from center. Steam peppers in 1 inch of water for 5 minutes. Cool. Brown ground beef. Drain off excess fat. Stir in Spanish rice and catsup. Spoon ingredients into green pepper halves. Place in baking pan and bake at 350 degrees for 25 minutes.

Cabbage and Beef Dish

Bake 350 Degrees   **1 Hour**

1) 1 pound lean ground beef
2) 1 medium onion, chopped
3) 3 cups cabbage, shredded
4) 1 can tomato soup

Brown ground beef and onion. Drain and season to taste. Spread in baking dish. Top with 3 cups cabbage. Pour tomato soup on top and cover. Bake at 350 degrees for 1 hour.

Casseroles are good time savers, as you can combine all the ingredients in one casserole and bake. Or, make two casseroles, one for now and the other for another day. Most casseroles freeze very well and can be frozen right in the container in which you cook it.

Beef and Cabbage Rolls

Stove Top
Bake 350 Degrees 10 to 12 Minutes

1)   1 pound lean ground beef
2)   1 medium onion, chopped
3)   1 cup sauerkraut, drained
4)   3 packages refrigerator crescent rolls

In a large skillet, brown beef and onions. Drain off any excess liquid. Season to taste. Add sauerkraut and cook until heated. Open crescent rolls and crimp 2 triangles together to form rectangles. Place small amount of meat mixture on each rectangle. Roll up. Slice each roll into 2 or 3 rounds. Place on greased baking sheet, cut side down. Bake at 350 degrees for 10 minutes or until browned.

Meat and Potato Dinner

Bake 350 Degrees   45 Minutes

1)   4 large potatoes, peeled and sliced
2)   1 pound lean ground beef, browned and drained
3)   Green peppers, sliced
4)   1 (28 ounce) can tomatoes, chopped

Layer above ingredients in order given. Bake at 350 degrees for 45 minutes.

Hot Meat Dish

Bake 350 Degrees   1 Hour

1)   1 1/2 pounds lean ground beef
2)   1 (6 ounce) package seasoned croutons
3)   2 cans cream of chicken soup
4)   1 soup can of milk

Pat ground beef into bottom of greased 9x12 casserole. Mix croutons, soup and milk. Pour over meat and bake at 350 degrees for 1 hour.

Vegetable Meat Dish

Bake 375 Degrees   1 Hour

1)   1 pound lean ground beef, browned and drained
2)   1 onion, chopped
3)   4 large potatoes, peeled and sliced
4)   1 (10 1/2 ounce) can vegetable beef soup

Brown ground beef and onions; drain. Place potato slices in lightly greased casserole. Spread ground beef and onions over potatoes. Pour soup over top. Cover and bake at 375 degrees for 45 minutes. Remove cover and continue baking 25 minutes.

Ground Beef and Pepper Skillet

Stove Top

1)   1 pound lean ground beef
2)   1 small onion, chopped
3)   1 green pepper, chopped
4)   1 (12 ounce) jar mushroom gravy

Brown ground beef, onion and green pepper. Drain. Add gravy and simmer for 20 to 30 minutes. Serve over rice or noodles.

Fiesta Dinner

Bake 350 Degrees   30 Minutes

1) 1 pound package taco flavored ground beef, browned and drained
2) 1 (16 ounce) can tomatoes, drained and chopped
3) 8 ounces Colby cheese, grated
4) 6 flour tortillas

Add tomatoes to taco meat. Simmer for 15 minutes. Layer one flour tortilla in round casserole. Place taco meat on tortilla and spread to cover. Sprinkle with cheese. Repeat layers starting with tortilla and ending with cheese. Bake at 350 degrees for 30 minutes.

Ranch Style Spaghetti

Bake 325 Degrees   45 Minutes

1) 1 pound lean ground beef, browned and drained
2) 1 (14 3/4 ounce) can spaghetti in tomato sauce
3) 1 (15 ounce) can ranch style beans
4) 8 ounces cheddar cheese, grated

Add spaghetti sauce and beans to browned meat. Place in casserole. Top with grated cheese. Bake at 325 degrees for 45 minutes.

Hamburger Sloppy Joes

Stove Top

1) 1 pound lean ground beef
2) 1/4 cup catsup
3) 1 tablespoon prepared mustard
4) 1 can chicken gumbo soup

Brown ground beef in skillet and drain. Combine ingredients. Simmer for 30 minutes. Serve between hamburger buns.

Beef Roast

Bake 500 Degrees 15 to 24 Minutes
2 hours with Oven Off

1) 3 to 4 pound eye of round roast
2) Cracked peppercorns
3) 1/4 teaspoon garlic salt (optional)
4) 1/4 teaspoon seasoned salt (optional)

Preheat oven to 500 degrees. Roll roast in peppercorns. Place in baking dish, then in preheated oven. Bake 5 to 6 minutes per pound. Turn oven off and leave roast in oven for 2 more hours. DO NOT OPEN OVEN DURING THIS TIME. Bake uncovered for medium done roast. Use juice to make gravy.

Mustard Onion Chuck Roast

Bake 325 Degrees   3 Hours

1) 2 tablespoons dry mustard
2) 1 1/2 teaspoons water
3) 3 pounds beef chuck pot roast
4) 1/2 cup soy sauce

Blend mustard with water to make a paste. Cover and let stand for 5 minutes. Place tin foil in shallow baking pan. Place meat on foil. Stir soy sauce into mustard mixture, blending until smooth. Pour mixture evenly over roast. Fold and seal foil to cover roast. Bake at 325 degrees for 3 hours.

Coke Roast

Bake 350 Degrees
30 Minutes per Pound

1) Beef Brisket or Roast
2) 1 package dry onion soup mix
3) 1 (12 ounce) jar chili sauce
4) 1 (12 ounce) can regular Coke

Mix soup, chili sauce and coke together. Pour over roast, cover and bake at 350 degrees for 30 minutes per pound. DO NOT USE FOIL WITH THIS BECAUSE OF COKE.

Beef Brisket

Bake 350 Degrees   3 Hours

1) 4 to 5 pounds beef brisket
2) 1/4 teaspoon garlic salt
3) 2 medium onions, sliced
4) 3 garlic cloves

Place brisket in roasting pan. Season with garlic salt. Place sliced onions and garlic cloves over top of roast. Bake covered at 350 degrees for 3 hours.

Easy Pot Roast

Stove Top

1)   3 to 4 pounds boneless beef pot roast
2)   1/4 cup oil
3)   1 can golden mushroom soup
4)   2 tablespoons flour paste (2 tablespoons flour blended
        with 1/4 cup cold water)

In heavy skillet, brown meat on all sides in oil. Stir in soup and
cover. Cook over low heat 3 hours, stirring occasionally. Remove
meat from skillet. To thicken pan gravy, add flour paste and stir
until smooth. Cook until thickened. Return meat to gravy until
ready to serve.

Oven Pot Roast and Gravy

Bake 350 Degrees
45 Minutes per Pound

1)   4 to 5 pounds pot roast
2)   1 package dry onion soup mix
3)   1 can mushroom soup
4)   1/4 teaspoon black pepper

Place roast in large heavy aluminum foil in baking pan. Shake
package of onion soup mix on top of pot roast. Cover roast with
mushroom soup. Close foil so steam does not escape, leaving an
air pocket above meat. Cook at 350 degrees about 45 minutes per
pound.

Sizzler Sirloin Steak

Grill or Broil

1) 3/4 cup catsup
2) 1/2 cup Worcestershire sauce
3) 1/3 cup oil
4) 3 pounds boneless beef sirloin steak

Mix catsup, Worcestershire sauce and oil together. Pour over steak and marinate overnight. Remove steak from marinade and grill on outdoor grill or broil in oven about 12 minutes on each side. Brush with marinade as it is cooking.

BBQ Flank Steak

Broil
8 Minutes per Side

1) 1 (32 ounce) package frozen French fries
2) 1 (16 ounce) package frozen onion rings
3) 1 (1 pound 2 ounce) bottle Hickory Smoke BBQ Sauce
4) 2 pounds tenderized flank steak

In shallow roasting pan (2 to 3 inches deep), mix potatoes and onion rings. Broil for 10 minutes. Remove from oven and stir and turn potatoes and onion rings. Drizzle with half the BBQ sauce. Top with flank steak. Cover any potatoes and onion rings that are not covered by the flank steak with foil. Return to oven and broil for 8 minutes, brushing steak with BBQ sauce. Turn steak, brush with BBQ sauce and broil another 8 minutes.

Chili Casserole

Bake 350 Degrees   **20 Minutes**

1)   1 (10 ounce) package tortilla chips, coarsely broken
2)   1 can nacho cheese soup, undiluted
3)   1 (15 ounce) can chili with beans
4)   1/4 teaspoon black pepper (optional)

Place 2 cups chips in lightly greased 1-quart baking dish. Spread half of cheese soup over chips. Spread all of the chili over soup. Season with black pepper if desired. Top with remaining cheese soup. Bake uncovered at 350 degrees for 15 minutes. Sprinkle with remaining chips. Bake 5 minutes longer.

Bean Boats

Bake 375 Degrees   **25 Minutes**

1)   2 (15 ounce) cans chili with beans
2)   4 French rolls
3)   1/4 cup margarine, melted
4)   1/2 cup shredded cheddar cheese

Cut tops off each French roll. Hollow out each roll reserving bread pieces. Brush inside and outside of rolls with margarine. Mix 1 cup of the bread pieces with chili and fill loaves. Replace tops of rolls and wrap in foil. Bake on cookie sheet at 375 degrees for 25 minutes. Remove tops and sprinkle with cheese. Replace tops and serve hot.

Flank Steak Supreme

Bake 350 Degrees   1 1/2 Hours

1) 1 tenderized flank steak
2) Onion salt
3) 1 (12 ounce) can mushroom gravy
4) 1/4 teaspoon black pepper (optional)

Preheat oven to 350 degrees. Place steak on aluminum foil in casserole. Season with onion salt and black pepper if desired. Spread mushroom gravy over steak. Roll steak. Wrap with foil and seal. Bake for 1 1/2 hours.

Chili Stuffed Peppers

Stove Top

1) 1 (15 ounce) can chili with beans
2) 4 small red or green peppers
3) 1 (11 ounce) can Mexican style corn, drained
4) Tortilla chips

Slice tops off of peppers. Remove inside and cook peppers gently in boiling water for 15 minutes. Drain. In a saucepan combine chili and corn and heat until boiling. Fill peppers and garnish with tortilla chips.

After removing a roast from the oven,
let it rest about 15 minutes for easier carving.

Broccoli Chicken

Bake 350 Degrees   1 Hour

1) 6 to 8 chicken breasts (boneless and skinless)
2) 2 (10 ounce) packages frozen broccoli
3) 1 can nacho cheese soup
4) 1/4 cup cooking sherry

In a skillet, brown chicken breasts and place in greased casserole. Mix broccoli, soup and sherry together. Pour over chicken and bake at 350 degrees uncovered for 1 hour.

Club Chicken

Bake 375 Degrees   1 Hour

1) 1 cup finely crushed Club or Town House Crackers
2) 1 package Italian salad dressing mix
3) 2 to 3 pounds frying chicken
4) 3 tablespoons margarine, melted

Combine cracker crumbs and salad dressing in large plastic bag. Shake 2 chicken pieces at a time in the crumb mixture. Place chicken, skin side up, in casserole dish. Drizzle with melted margarine. Bake for 1 hour at 375 degrees.

Chicken Risotto

Stove Top

1) 2 1/2 pounds frying chicken, cut up
2) 1 (7 1/2 ounce) package Rice-a-Roni (any flavor)
3) 1 can chicken broth plus water to equal 2 1/4 cups liquid
4) 1 (3 ounce) jar pimiento stuffed olives, drained

In a skillet, brown chicken (about 10 minutes on each side). Remove chicken from skillet leaving grease in pan. Add rice, including seasoning packet, to skillet and stir until lightly browned. Pour in chicken broth and water. Bring mixture to a boil. Place chicken on top of rice mixture. Lower heat, cover and simmer 20 to 30 minutes. Fluff rice with fork and top with olives.

Cherry Sherry Chicken

Bake 350 Degrees   1 to 1 1/2 Hours

1) 4 to 6 chicken breasts
2) 2 cups cooking sherry
3) 1 (16 ounce) can tart pitted cherries, drained
4) 1 tablespoon sugar (optional)

Pour sherry and cherries over chicken pieces, cover and bake for 1 to 1 1/2 hours at 325 degrees.

Nutty Chicken

Bake 350 Degrees   **1 Hour**

1) 1 cup biscuit mix, mixed in 1 cup water
2) 1 (3.75 ounce) package salted roasted sunflower nuts, chopped
3) 3 to 4 pounds chicken pieces
4) Vegetable oil

Combine biscuit mix, water and nuts. Dip chicken in batter and brown in hot oil until golden. Place chicken in shallow baking dish and bake for 1 hour at 350 degrees.

Chicken Wild Rice Casserole

Bake 375 Degrees   **45 Minutes**

1) 1 (6 ounce) package wild rice, cooked
2) 2 cups chicken meat, cooked, boned and cubed
3) 2 cans cream of mushroom soup
4) 1/3 cup chicken broth

Prepare rice as directed on package. Mix all the above ingredients and bake for 45 minutes at 375 degrees.

Swiss Chicken Casserole

Bake 350 Degrees   **1 Hour**

1) 6 chicken breasts (skinless and boneless)
2) 6 slices Swiss cheese
3) 1 can cream of chicken soup, undiluted
4) 1/4 cup milk

Place chicken in greased casserole. Top with cheese. Mix soup and milk; stir well. Spoon over chicken and cover. Bake for 1 hour at 350 degrees.

Chicken Spinach Bake

Bake 400 Degrees   **15 Minutes**

1) 1 (8 ounce) package fine egg noodles
2) 1 (9 ounce) package frozen creamed spinach, thawed
3) 1 tablespoon vegetable oil
4) 1 1/2 cups chicken, cooked and cubed

Cook noodles and drain. Coat 9x9-inch baking dish with cooking spray. Turn noodles into dish and stir in spinach and oil. Top with chicken and bake for 15 minutes at 400 degrees.

Honey Mustard Chicken

Broil   **8 to 10 Minutes per Side**

1) 1/2 cup Miracle Whip salad dressing
2) 2 tablespoons Dijon mustard
3) 1 tablespoon honey
4) 4 chicken breasts (skinless and boneless)

Combine salad dressing, mustard and honey. Brush chicken with 1/2 of mixture and broil 8 to 10 minutes per side. After turning chicken, baste with remaining mixture.

To test chicken for doneness, pierce a meaty portion.
Meat should be tender and moist with no pink tinge.
Meat juices should be clear.

Italian Chicken

Stove Top

1) 6 to 8 chicken breasts (skinless and boneless)
2) 2 tablespoons vegetable oil
3) 1 cup chopped onion
4) 1 (14 ounce) jar spaghetti sauce with mushrooms

Brown chicken in oil. Push to one side and saute onions until tender. Stir in spaghetti sauce and cover skillet. Simmer for 25 minutes or until chicken is tender. Serve with pasta.

Zesty Crisp Chicken

Bake 350 Degrees   1 Hour

1) 4 chicken breasts (boneless and skinless)
2) 1 egg, slightly beaten
3) 1/4 cup soy sauce
4) 1 1/4 cups corn flakes, crushed

Mix egg and soy sauce. Dip chicken pieces in soy sauce mixture. Coat with corn flake crumbs. Place on baking sheet and bake for 1 hour at 350 degrees.

Herb Lemon Chicken

Stove Top

1) 4 chicken breasts (boneless and skinless)
2) 1 egg, beaten
3) All purpose flour
4) 1 package Lipton Golden Herb with Lemon Mix, mixed with 1 cup water

Dip chicken in egg, then flour. Place in large skillet and brown in oil over medium heat. Add soup mix and bring to a boil. Cover and simmer 30 minutes or until chicken is cooked.

Potato Mustard Chicken

Bake 400 Degrees   **45 Minutes**

1)   **4 chicken breasts**
2)   **2 cups potatoes, shredded**
3)   **1 onion, sliced**
4)   **1/2 cup honey mustard prepared dressing**

Spread shredded potatoes in bottom of 9x12-inch lightly greased casserole. Place sliced onion on top of potatoes. Place chicken breasts on top of onions and drizzle salad dressing over chicken breasts. Bake 45 minutes at 400 degrees. Season to taste.

Fiesta Chicken

Bake 350 Degrees   **1 Hour**

1)   **4 chicken breasts (boneless and skinless)**
2)   **1/2 cup yogurt**
3)   **2 tablespoons taco seasoning mix**
4)   **1 cup cheddar cheese cracker crumbs**

Coat chicken breasts with yogurt. Combine cracker crumbs and taco seasoning. Dredge chicken in mixture. Place in greased baking dish. Bake uncovered 350 degrees for 1 hour.

For quick seasoning while cooking, keep a large shaker containing six parts salt to one part pepper.

Onion Ring Chicken

Bake 350 Degrees   45 Minutes

1) 4 chicken breasts (skinless and boneless)
2) 1/2 cup margarine, melted
3) 1 tablespoon Worcestershire sauce
4) 1 (2.5 ounce) can fried onion rings, crushed

Flatten each breast, season to taste. Combine margarine and Worcestershire sauce. Dredge chicken in margarine mixture, then crushed onion rings. Arrange in baking pan. Top with any remaining margarine mixture. Bake at 350 degrees for 45 minutes or until tender.

Pecan Chicken

Bake 350 Degrees   1 Hour

1) 1/4 cup honey
2) 1/4 cup Dijon mustard
3) 4 chicken breasts (skinned, boned and halved)
4) 1 cup pecans, finely ground

Combine honey and mustard. Spread on both sides of chicken. Dredge chicken in chopped pecans. Place in lightly greased baking dish. Bake at 350 degrees for 1 hour or until tender.

Confetti Chicken

Stove Top

1) 1 1/2 cups chicken, cooked and cubed
2) 2 (14 1/2 ounce) cans seasoned tomatoes/onions
3) 1 green pepper, chopped
4) 2 cups rice, cooked

In skillet, combine first three ingredients and season to taste. Simmer for 10 to 15 minutes. Serve over rice.

Tangy Chicken

Stove Top

1) 2 1/2 pounds chicken (cut-up)
2) 2 tablespoons margarine
3) 1/2 cup Heinz 57 sauce
4) 1/2 cup water

In skillet, brown chicken in margarine. Combine sauce and water and pour over chicken. Cover and simmer for 40 minutes or until chicken is tender. Baste occasionally. Remove cover last 10 minutes of cooking. Spoon sauce over chicken before serving.

Baked Chicken and Beans

Bake 350 Degrees   50 Minutes

1) 4 chicken breasts
2) 1 can cream of mushroom soup
3) 1 (12 ounce) can cut green beans, drained
4) 1 (16 ounce) package frozen onion rings

Place chicken in greased casserole and cover with soup. Bake for 30 minutes at 350 degrees. Place beans in casserole with chicken. Top with onion rings. Bake for 20 minutes longer or until chicken is tender and onion rings are crisp and brown.

Chicken Noodle Casserole

Bake 350 Degrees   **1 Hour**

1) 1 (8 ounce) package egg noodles, cooked and drained
2) 1 can cream of mushroom soup, undiluted
3) 6 chicken legs or thighs
4) Paprika

Combine cooked noodles and soup. Place into a casserole. Arrange chicken on top of noodles. Sprinkle with paprika. Cover and bake at 350 degrees for 1 hour or until chicken is tender.

Hawaiian Chicken

Stove Top

1) 10 ounces breaded chicken tenders
2) 1 (10 ounce) jar sweet and sour sauce
3) 1 (8 3/4 ounce) can pineapple tidbits
4) 1 (16 ounce) package frozen Oriental vegetables

Prepare chicken tenders according to package directions. Place tenders in large skillet. Add sweet and sour sauce, pineapple and vegetables. Cover and simmer 25 minutes or until vegetables are tender. Serve over rice.

Chicken Meat Balls

Stove Top

1) 1 pound ground chicken
2) 1 egg, slightly beaten
3) 2/3 cup corn bread stuffing mix
4) 2 tablespoons sour cream

Combine chicken, egg and stuffing mix. Shape into 16 meat balls.
Lightly coat skillet with cooking spray and brown meat balls.
Reduce heat to low and add 1/4 cup water. Cover and simmer for
15 minutes. Stir a little cooking liquid into sour cream and then
stir back into skillet. Gently heat to serving temperature. Add
2 to 4 more tablespoons water, if necessary.

Turkey Roll-Ups

Stove Top   Bake 350 Degrees
                      25 to 30 Minutes

1) 1 (6 ounce) box Stove Top dressing
2) 1/4 cup margarine plus 1 2/3 cups water
3) 6 slices "Deli" turkey, medium thickness
4) 1 (12 ounce) can chicken gravy

Prepare dressing mix as directed with margarine and water.
Spoon dressing onto slice of turkey and roll up. Place seam side
down in casserole. Repeat until all slices are "stuffed". Pour gravy
over the top of turkey and dressing. Bake for 25 to 30 minutes at
350 degrees.

Spicy Chops

Broil

1)   4 (1/2 inch thick) boneless pork loin chops
2)   1/4 cup picante
3)   2 tablespoons water
4)   2 tablespoons marmalade

Place pork chops in baking dish. Mix picante, water and marmalade. Pour over chops, turning to coat. Marinate about 1 hour. Broil chops about 8 to 10 minutes per side, basting with leftover marinade.

Pork Chops with Red Cabbage

Stove Top

1)   4 (1 inch thick) loin pork chops
2)   1 large onion, chopped
3)   1 (15 ounce) jar sweet/sour red cabbage
4)   1 apple, quartered, cored and sliced

Brown pork chops in non-stick skillet. Remove chops. Saute onion until tender. Arrange chops over onions. Place cabbage and apple slices over top of pork chops. Cover and simmer for 30 minutes or until chops are cooked thoroughly.

The main rule to keep in mind when cooking pork is to cook it thoroughly.

Pork Stir Fry

Stove Top

1) 2 boneless pork loin chops, cut into 1/4 inch strips
2) 1 (14 ounce) bag frozen Oriental stir-fry vegetables/ seasoning pack
3) 1 tablespoon soy sauce
4) 2 teaspoons vegetable oil

Coat large skillet with cooking spray. Heat to medium-high temperature and add pork strips. Stir-fry 3 minutes or until no longer pink. Add vegetables, cover and cook 5 minutes. Add 1/4 cup water, vegetable seasoning packet, soy sauce and oil. Cook, stirring until mixture is heated through. Serve over rice.

Saucy Pork Chops

Bake 350 Degrees   1 Hour

1) 6 pork chops
2) 1 cup applesauce
3) 1/4 cup soy sauce
4) 1/8 teaspoon onion powder

Brown pork chops on both sides. Place in shallow casserole. Combine remaining ingredients and spoon evenly over chops. Cover and bake at 350 degrees for 45 minutes. Remove cover and continue baking 15 minutes longer or until chops are tender.

Pork Chop Casserole Supper

Bake 350 Degrees   1 Hour

1)   4 pork chops
2)   1 (16 ounce) can peas (reserve liquid)
3)   1 can cream of mushroom soup
4)   1/4 cup chopped onion

Arrange pork chops in casserole. Combine peas, 1/4 cup of the pea liquid, soup and onion. Pour over pork chops and cover. Bake 50 minutes at 350 degrees; uncover and bake an additional 10 minutes.

Oven Fried Pork Chops

Bake 425 Degrees 30 to 45 Minutes

1)   3 tablespoons margarine, melted
2)   1 egg plus 2 tablespoons water, beaten
3)   1 cup cornbread stuffing mix
4)   4 pork chops

Place margarine in 13x9-inch baking pan. Dip pork chops in egg mixture, then stuffing mix to coat. Place chops on top of melted margarine. Bake for 20 minutes at 425 degrees, turn and bake 10 to 15 minutes more or until browned.

Tex-Mex Chops

Stove Top

1)   4 boneless pork chops
2)   1 tablespoon vegetable oil
3)   1 cup salsa
4)   Salt and pepper to taste (optional)

Season pork chops to taste. In skillet, brown both sides of chops in oil. Add salsa and lower heat. Simmer 30 minutes or until chops are thoroughly cooked.

Mustard-Apricot Pork Chops

Broil

1)   1/3 cup apricot preserves
2)   2 tablespoons Dijon mustard
3)   4 (3/4 inch) pork chops
4)   3 green onions, chopped

Combine preserves and mustard in small saucepan. Heat until preserves melt, stirring. Set aside. Place chops on lightly greased broiler pan. Broil 5 minutes. Brush chops with half of the glaze and turn. Broil 5 minutes longer. Turn and brush with remaining glaze. Broil 2 minutes. Garnish with green onions before serving.

Grilled Pork Chops

Grill

1)   1/4 teaspoon salt
2)   3/4 teaspoon lemon pepper
3)   1/2 teaspoon dried whole oregano leaves
4)   4 (1-inch thick) pork chops

Mix salt, lemon pepper and oregano. Coat pork chops. Grill over low to medium hot heat for 25 minutes or until chops are no longer pink. Turn once.

Honey Glazed Ham

Bake 325 Degrees   **2 1/2 Hours**

1)   10 pound ham
2)   1/2 cup honey
3)   1/3 cup brown sugar
4)   1/4 cup orange juice

Score ham. Mix honey, brown sugar and orange juice together. Rub mixture over scored ham and place fat side up in roasting pan. Bake at 325 degrees for 2 1/2 hours. Last 30 minutes, baste with juices.

Ham in Madeira Wine

Stove Top

1)   10 pound ham
2)   4 bay leaves
3)   8 peppercorns
4)   1 bottle Madeira wine

Soak ham in cold water overnight. Drain. In large pot, cover drained ham in boiling water. Add bay leaves and peppercorns and cook slowly 2 1/2 hours. Drain off liquid. Pour wine over ham and simmer at least 1/2 hour, basting with wine. Slice and serve.

Oven Braised Ham

Bake 350 Degrees   **30 Minutes**

1)   6 (1/4 inch thick) slices cooked ham
2)   2 tablespoons brown sugar
3)   1/4 cup water
4)   Pineapple slices (optional)

Place ham in lightly greased casserole. Cover with pineapple slices if desired. Sprinkle with brown sugar. Pour water around ham. Cover and bake at 350 degrees for 30 minutes.

Ham with Red-Eye Gravy

1) 6 (1/4 inch thick) slices country ham
2) 1/4 cup margarine
3) 1/4 cup firmly packed brown sugar
4) 1/2 cup strong black coffee

Saute ham in margarine over low heat until light brown, turning several times. Remove ham from skillet, cover with foil to keep warm. Stir sugar into pan drippings and heat until sugar dissolves, stirring constantly. Add coffee and simmer 5 minutes. Season gravy to taste. Serve over ham slices.

Roman Spaghetti

Stove Top

1) 1/2 pound lean bacon, diced
2) 1/4 cup margarine
3) 1 pound spaghetti noodles, cooked and drained
4) 2/3 cup Romano cheese

Melt margarine in saucepan and cook bacon until crisp. Remove bacon, retain bacon grease and margarine. Place spaghetti in serving bowl. Toss half of the bacon grease/margarine mixture with the spaghetti. Sprinkle with bacon and cheese and serve.

Sausage Bake

Bake 350 Degrees   45 Minutes

1)   1 pound Polish sausage, cut into 1-inch pieces
2)   1 cup shredded cheese
3)   1 cup sliced celery
4)   2 (10 3/4 ounce) cans cream of mushroom soup

Combine all ingredients and place in 2-quart casserole. Bake covered 45 minutes at 350 degrees.

Franks and Crescents

Bake 375 Degrees 10 to 12 Minutes

1)   8 hot dogs, partially split along length
2)   Cheddar cheese, cut in strips
3)   1 (8 ounce) can refrigerated crescent dinner rolls
4)   Mustard on the side (optional)

Fill each hot dog with strip of cheese. Separate crescent dough into 8 triangles. Place hot dog on each triangle and roll up. Place on greased cookie sheet (cheese side up) and bake at 375 degrees for 10 to 12 minutes. Serve with mustard if desired.

Hot Dog Tacos

Stove Top

1)   4 hot dogs, finely chopped
2)   2 ounces Velveeta cheese, cubed
3)   1/3 cup picante
4)   Flour tortillas, warmed

Place first 3 ingredients in non-stick skillet. Heat over low heat until cheese is melted. Place mixture in flour tortilla and roll up.

Baked Orange Roughy

Bake 400 Degrees   **25 Minutes**

1)   **1 pound orange roughy fillets**
2)   **1/4 cup lemon juice**
3)   **1/2 teaspoon tarragon leaves**
4)   **2 teaspoons dried mustard**

Place fillets in large casserole. Squeeze lemon juice over fillets. Sprinkle dried mustard and tarragon leaves over fish. Bake at 400 degrees for 25 minutes.

Buttermilk Fried Fillets

Stove Top

1)   **2 pounds skinless fish fillets**
2)   **1 cup buttermilk**
3)   **1 cup Bisquick mix**
4)   **Cooking oil**

Place fish in shallow dish. Pour buttermilk over fish and let it marinate for 30 minutes, turning once. Roll fish in Bisquick mix, season to taste and fry in hot oil 4 to 5 minutes on each side.

You should not thaw fish at room temperature or in warm water. It will lose moisture and flavor. Instead, thaw fish in the refrigerator.

Spanish Fish

Bake 350 Degrees
20 Minutes per Pound

1)   1 fish (snapper or redfish)
2)   1 bell pepper, chopped
3)   1 red onion, chopped
4)   1 (14 1/2 ounce) can seasoned tomatoes

Line shallow pan with foil leaving ample amount hanging over the edges. Pour 1/3 of the tomatoes onto the foil. Place fish over tomatoes. Sprinkle the bell pepper and onion over the fish. Pour remaining tomatoes over fish and loosely close up foil. Bake at 350 degrees for 20 minutes per pound or until fish is flaky.

Cordon Bleu Fish Fillets

Bake 400 Degrees   **2 to 3 Minutes**

1)   1 (8 ounce) package fried fish fillets
2)   4 slices boiled ham
3)   4 slices Swiss cheese
4)   1 can cream of mushroom soup, plus 1/2 soup can water

Prepare fish according to package directions. Top each cooked fillet with a slice of ham and cheese. Return to 400 degree oven for 2 to 3 minutes until cheese is partially melted. Combine soup and water in small saucepan and heat thoroughly. Pour over fish and serve.

Caesar's Fish

Bake 400 Degrees   15 Minutes

1) 1 pound flounder fillets
2) 1/2 cup prepared Caesar's salad dressing
3) 1 cup round buttery cracker crumbs
4) 1/2 cup shredded cheddar cheese

Place fillets in lightly greased casserole dish. Drizzle Caesar dressing over fillets. Sprinkle cracker crumbs over top of fillets. Bake at 400 degrees for 10 minutes. Top with cheese and bake an additional 5 minutes or until fish flakes easily with fork.

Lemon Dill Fish

Broil   5 to 8 Minutes per side

1) 1 pound fish fillets
2) 1/2 cup Miracle Whip
3) 2 tablespoons lemon juice
4) 1 teaspoon dillweed

Combine Miracle Whip, lemon juice and dill. Place fish in broiler pan. Brush with sauce. Broil 5 to 8 minutes, turn once and brush with sauce. Continuing broiling for 5 to 8 minutes.

As a rule, thawed fish should not be kept longer than one day before cooking. The flavor is better if it is cooked immediately after thawing.

Trout Almondine

Bake 350 Degrees   **25 Minutes**

1) 2 trout fillets
2) 1/3 cup slivered almonds
3) 1 tablespoon butter, melted
4) 1/2 teaspoon chopped parsley

Arrange almonds on ungreased cookie sheet and bake for 4 to 5 minutes at 350 degrees. Set aside. Place fish on ungreased baking sheet. Combine almonds, butter and parsley. Spoon over fish. Bake uncovered at 350 degrees for 25 minutes.

Italian Scallops

Stove Top

1) 1 tablespoon butter
2) 1 tablespoon garlic powder
3) 1/2 tablespoon Italian herbs
4) 1 pound fresh sea scallops

Melt butter in large skillet. Add garlic powder, scallops and Italian herbs. Cook over medium-high heat, stirring constantly, 6 to 8 minutes.

Pepper Shrimp

Bake 350 Degrees   **30 Minutes**

1) 1 pound jumbo shrimp in shells
2) 1/2 cup butter, melted
3) 3 tablespoons Worcestershire sauce
4) 3 tablespoons fresh ground pepper

Arrange shrimp in one layer in flat pan. Combine butter, Worcestershire sauce and pepper. Pour sauce mixture over shrimp and stir. Bake uncovered at 350 degrees for 30 minutes. Stir often.

Marinated Grilled Shrimp

Grill or Broil

1) 2 tablespoons soy sauce
2) 2 tablespoons vegetable oil
3) 1 tablespoon honey
4) 1 pound large shrimp, peeled and deveined

Mix soy sauce, oil and honey and pour over shrimp. Marinate at least 1 hour. Place on skewers and grill or broil 4 to 5 minutes until cooked through and browned.

Shrimp Marinara

Stove Top

1) 1 clove garlic, minced
2) 1 tablespoon vegetable oil
3) 1 (1 pound 12 ounce) can Italian style tomatoes
4) 1 pound frozen shrimp, shelled and deveined

Saute garlic in oil until tender. Add tomatoes and cook until sauce thickens and tomatoes break up, about 20 minutes. Add shrimp and cook 5 more minutes. Serve over rice.

Easy Crab Dish

Broil   **12 to 15 Minutes**

1) 1 pound lump blue crab meat (fresh or frozen)
2) 1/2 cup margarine, melted
3) 1 tablespoon vinegar
4) 1 teaspoon tarragon

Thaw frozen crab meat. Drain. Place crab meat in shallow casserole. Combine margarine and vinegar and pour over crab. Sprinkle with tarragon. Toss. Broil 12 to 15 minutes or until lightly browned.

Bacon Crisp Oysters

Broil

1) 1 (12 ounce) jar fresh oysters, drained
2) 8 slices bacon, cut into thirds
3) 2 tablespoons parsley
4) Salt and pepper

Place one oyster on each piece of bacon. Sprinkle with parsley, salt and pepper. Wrap bacon around oyster and secure with toothpick. Place broiler rack 4 inches from heat and broil 8 minutes on one side. Turn and broil 5 minutes on other side. Bacon will be crisp and oysters will curl.

Oyster Sausage Stew

Stove Top

1) 1/2 pound pork sausage
2) 1/2 cup diced onion
3) 1 (12 ounce) container fresh oysters
4) 1 1/2 cups milk

Brown sausage and onion. Remove from skillet. Place oysters with liquid in skillet and cook over low heat until edges curl. Turn. Return sausage and onion to skillet. Stir in milk. Simmer until thoroughly heated.

Grilled Tuna Steaks

Grill or Broil   5 Minutes per Side

1)   4 tuna steaks
2)   1 cup prepared Italian salad dressing
3)   2 teaspoons fresh ground pepper
4)   1 lemon

Place steaks in casserole. Pour dressing over tuna. Cover and
refrigerate for 1 hour, turning once. Remove steaks from
marinade and sprinkle pepper on both sides. Grill or broil
5 minutes on each side. Squeeze lemon over steaks and serve.

Quick Tuna Casserole

Bake 350 Degrees   20 Minutes

1)   1 (6 1/2 ounce) can tuna, drained
2)   3 cups Rice Krispies
3)   1 can cream of mushroom soup
4)   1 can chicken noodle soup

Mix above ingredients and bake at 350 degrees for 20 minutes.

Broccoli Tuna Casserole

Bake 350 Degrees   1 Hour

1)   1 (6 1/2 ounce) can tuna, drained
2)   1 (10 ounce) package frozen chopped broccoli, thawed
         and drained
3)   1 can mushroom soup
4)   1 cup crushed seasoned potato chips

Layer tuna, broccoli and mushroom soup in small baking dish.
Cover with crushed potato chips. Bake, uncovered, at 350 degrees
for 1 hour.

Tater Tot Tuna

Bake 300 Degrees   20 Minutes

1)   2 (6 1/2 ounce) cans tuna, drained
2)   1 can cream of chicken soup
3)   1 (16 ounce) can French-style green beans, drained
4)   1 (16 ounce) package Tater Tots

Combine tuna with soup and green beans. Place in casserole dish.
Brown Tater Tots in oven according to package directions. Place
Tater Tots on top of tuna mixture. Bake at 300 degrees for
20 minutes or until mixture is bubbly.

Quick Tuna Pot Pie

Bake 425 Degrees   15 Minutes

1)   1 (6 1/2 ounce) can tuna, drained
2)   1 can mushroom soup
3)   1 (16 ounce) can peas, drained
4)   1 can refrigerator biscuits

Combine tuna, soup and peas. Place in greased casserole. Arrange
biscuits on top of mixture. Bake at 425 degrees for 15 minutes or
until biscuits are golden brown.

Desserts

Pineapple-Lemon Pie

Graham Cracker Crust

1) 1 (6 ounce) can frozen lemonade
2) 1 (14 ounce) can sweetened condensed milk
3) 1 (8 ounce) carton Cool Whip
4) 1 (15 1/4 ounce) can crushed pineapple, drained

Mix above ingredients and pour into graham cracker crust. Freeze until ready to serve.

Blueberry Pie

Graham Cracker Crust

1) 1 (1 pound 6 ounce) can blueberry pie filling
2) 1 (8 ounce) carton Cool Whip
3) 1 (8 ounce) package cream cheese, softened
4) Sprinkle graham cracker crumbs (optional)

Place pie filling in graham cracker crust. Combine softened cream cheese with Cool Whip and spread over pie filling. Sprinkle with crumbs if desired. Chill at least 1 hour before serving.

Key Lime Pie

Unbaked Pie Shell

1) 6 egg yolks
2) 2 (14 ounce) cans sweetened condensed milk
3) 1 cup Realime lime juice from concentrate
4) Green food coloring (optional)

Combine and beat above ingredients. Pour into pie shell. Bake at 325 degrees for 40 minutes. Cool and chill in refrigerator before serving.

Margarita Pie

Graham Cracker Crust

1)   1 (8 ounce) package cream cheese, softened
2)   2 packages Holland House Margarita Mix
3)   1/2 to 3/4 cup sugar
4)   1 (8 ounce) carton Cool Whip

Cream the cream cheese until fluffy. Add margarita mix and sugar and beat until smooth. Add Cool Whip and mix. Freeze in graham cracker crust until ready to serve.

Koolaid Pie

Graham Cracker Crust

1)   1 (12 ounce) can evaporated milk, refrigerated so it is cold
2)   2/3 cup sugar
3)   1 (.15 ounce) package Koolaid (any flavor)
4)   Cool Whip (optional)

Beat milk until it is doubled in size. Add sugar and Koolaid and beat until thickened (about 5 minutes). Place in graham cracker crust and refrigerate until ready to serve. Top with Cool Whip if desired.

Vanilla Sour Cream Pie

Baked Pie Shell

1)   1 cup sour cream
2)   1 cup milk
3)   1 (3 1/2 ounce) package vanilla instant pudding
4)   Cool Whip (optional)

Beat sour cream and milk until smooth. Beat in dry pudding mix until smooth and slightly thickened. Pour into pie crust and chill 1 hour or until set. Serve topped with Cool Whip if desired.

Cookie Crust Ice Cream Pie

1) 1 (18 ounce) roll refrigerator chocolate chip cookies
2) 1 quart chocolate ice cream, softened
3) 1 (12 ounce) jar chocolate fudge sauce
4) 1 (8 ounce) carton Cool Whip

Slice cookie dough 1/8-inch thick. Line bottom and sides of 9-inch pie pan with cookie slices, overlapping sides to make scalloped edge. Bake 10 minutes at 375 degrees. Cool. Fill cooled crust with ice cream. Top with syrup and frost with Cool Whip. Freeze. To serve, cut into wedges.

Butter Pecan Pie

Graham Cracker Crust

1) 1 1/2 cups butter pecan ice cream, softened
2) 2 (1 1/2 ounce) English toffee flavored candy bars, crushed
3) 1 1/2 cups vanilla ice cream, softened
4) Cool Whip (optional)

Spread butter pecan ice cream in graham cracker crust. Sprinkle with half of crushed candy bar. Freeze. Spread vanilla ice cream over top of crushed candy bar. Sprinkle with remaining candy and freeze until ready to serve. Top with Cool Whip if desired.

Peanut Butter Pie

Graham Cracker Crust

1) 1 (8 ounce) package cream cheese, softened
2) 1 cup powdered sugar
3) 1 cup crunchy peanut butter
4) 1 (8 ounce) carton Cool Whip

Cream the cream cheese. Add sugar and peanut butter. Beat until smooth. Fold in Cool Whip. Place in graham cracker crust. Refrigerate or freeze.

Strawberry Pie

Baked Pie Shell

1) 1 tablespoon strawberry Jello, plus 1 cup hot water
2) 3 tablespoons cornstarch
3) 1 cup sugar
4) 1 pint fresh strawberries, sliced

Mix first 3 ingredients in saucepan and cook over medium heat until thick. Remove from heat and stir in strawberries. Cool. Pour into baked pie shell. Refrigerate.

Strawberry Mallow Pie

Baked Pie Shell

1) 1 (10 ounce) package frozen sweetened strawberries, thawed
2) 20 large marshmallows
3) 1 (8 ounce) carton Cool Whip
4) Baked pie shell

Heat strawberry juice in pan and slowly add marshmallows. Stir until marshmallows are melted. Cool. Fold in Cool Whip and strawberries. Mix well. Pour into pie shell and refrigerate.

Strawberry Yogurt Pie

Graham Cracker Crust

1) 2 cups strawberry yogurt
2) 1/2 cup strawberry preserves
3) 1 (8 ounce) carton Cool Whip, thawed
4) Graham cracker crust

Combine strawberry preserves and yogurt in bowl. Fold in Cool Whip. Spoon into graham cracker crust and freeze. Remove and place in refrigerator for 30 minutes before serving.

German Chocolate Pie

Baked Chocolate Pie Shell

1) 1 (4 ounce) package Baker's German Sweet Chocolate
2) 1/3 cup milk
3) 1 (3 ounce) package cream cheese, softened
4) 1 (8 ounce) carton Cool Whip

Heat chocolate and 2 tablespoons milk over low heat. Stir until melted. Remove from heat. Beat cream cheese and add remaining milk and chocolate mixture. Beat until smooth. Fold Cool Whip into chocolate mixture and blend until smooth. Spoon into crust. Freeze about 4 hours before serving.

Frozen unbaked pie shells do not need to be thawed and can go right into oven.

Malted Milk Pie

Baked Graham Cracker Crust

1) 1 pint vanilla ice cream, softened
2) 1 1/2 cups malted milk balls, crushed
3) 1 (8 ounce) carton Cool Whip
4) 1/3 cup marshmallow topping

Combine ice cream with 1/2 cup crushed malted milk balls. Spread mixture into graham cracker crust. Freeze. Blend marshmallow topping with 3/4 cup crushed malted milk balls. Fold into Cool Whip. Spread over frozen ice cream layer. Freeze several hours. Top with remaining 1/4 cup crushed malted balls.

Angel Nut Cake

1) 7 egg whites
2) 1 1/2 cups ground nuts
3) 1 1/2 cups powdered sugar, sifted
4) 1/8 teaspoon cream of tartar (optional)

Beat egg whites until stiff. Fold in nuts and sugar and add cream of tartar if desired. Bake in greased tube pan or flat cake pan for about 45 minutes at 350 degrees. See Angel Nut Frosting.

Angel Nut Frosting

1) 5 tablespoons milk
2) 1 cup sugar
3) 5 tablespoons butter
4) 1/2 cup chocolate chips

In saucepan, melt butter; add sugar and milk. Bring to a boil, stir 1 minute or until slightly thick. Fold in chocolate chips. Frost cake.

Butter Cake

1) 1 cup butter, softened
2) 2 cups flour
3) 1 cup sugar
4) 1 egg, slightly beaten

Mix ingredients. Place dough in greased and floured round cake pan. Bake at 375 degrees for 30 minutes. Serve warm with fresh fruit.

Lemon Cake

1) 1 package lemon pudding cake mix
2) 2/3 cup oil
3) 4 eggs
4) 1 1/4 cups 7-Up

Mix cake and oil. Beat. Add eggs one at a time. Add 7-Up; beat. Pour into a greased and floured 13x9-inch cake pan. Bake at 350 degrees for 30 minutes.

Lemon Cake Frosting

1) 1 (8 ounce) carton Cool Whip
2) 1 (8 ounce) can crushed pineapple, drained
3) 1 cup coconut
4) 2 tablespoons powdered sugar (optional)

Mix above ingredients and frost cake. Refrigerate until ready to serve.

Tomato Spice Cake

1)   1 package spice cake mix
2)   1 (10 ounce) can tomato soup, plus 1/4 cup water
3)   3 eggs
4)   1/3 cup vegetable oil

Combine ingredients in large bowl. Beat at low speed until moistened. Beat at medium speed for 2 minutes. Pour batter into 9x13-inch cake pan and bake at 350 degrees for 30 to 35 minutes.

Rich Chocolate Cake

1)   1 package devil's food cake mix
2)   3 eggs
3)   1 1/3 cup water
4)   1 cup Miracle Whip

Mix above ingredients. Place in greased 9x13-inch cake pan. Bake at 350 degrees for 40 minutes.

Cake Tip: For best results in cake baking, let eggs, butter and milk reach room temperature before mixing.

Ugly Duckling Cake

1) 1 box yellow cake mix
2) 1 (17 ounce) can fruit cocktail with syrup
3) 1 cup coconut
4) 2 eggs

Blend above ingredients. Beat 2 minutes at medium speed.
Pour into a greased 9x13-inch cake pan. Bake at 350 degrees for
45 minutes.

Ugly Duckling Frosting

1) 1 cup brown sugar
2) 1/4 cup evaporated milk
3) 1 stick margarine
4) 1 cup coconut

In saucepan, combine brown sugar, milk and margarine. Cook
5 minutes over medium heat, stirring constantly. Remove from
heat and stir in coconut. Pour over cake.

Festive Cranberry Cake

1) 1 angel food cake, prepared
2) 1 1/2 cups chilled whipping cream
3) 1/3 cup confectioners sugar
4) 1 (14 ounce) jar cranberry-orange relish

Split cake to make 4 layers. In chilled bowl, beat whipping cream
and sugar until stiff. Stack layers spreading each with a fourth of
the whipped cream mixture, then a fourth of the cranberry-
orange relish. Swirl it into whipped cream. Refrigerate cake
1 to 2 hours before serving.

Triple Fudge Cake

1) 1 (4 ounce) package chocolate pudding and pie filling
2) 2 cups milk
3) 1 package devil's food cake mix
4) 1/2 cup semi-sweet chocolate chips

Cook chocolate pudding in 2 cups milk. Blend cake mix into hot pudding, beating by hand or with mixer for 2 minutes. Pour into greased and floured 9x13-inch cake pan. Sprinkle batter with chocolate chips. Bake at 350 degrees for 35 minutes. If desired, top with whipped cream.

Apricot Cake

1) 1 yellow cake mix
2) 4 egg whites
3) 1/2 cup Canola Oil
4) 1 cup apricot nectar

Spray bundt pan with vegetable oil spray. Mix above ingredients and pour into pan. Bake at 350 degrees for 30 minutes. Best if it is slightly undercooked.

Almond Bark Cookies

1) 1 (24 ounce) package almond bark
2) 1 cup peanut butter
3) 8 cups Captain Krunch cereal
4) 1 cup salted peanuts

Melt almond bark according to package directions. Add peanut butter and mix. Remove from heat and stir in cereal and peanuts. Drop by spoonfuls onto wax paper. Cool.

Coconut Cookies

1)   1 (14 ounce) package coconut
2)   1 (12 ounce) package semi-sweet chocolate chips
3)   1 (14 ounce) can sweetened condensed milk
4)   1/4 cup chopped pecans (optional)

Mix ingredients. Drop by tablespoonful onto lightly greased cookie sheet. Bake at 325 degrees for 13 to 15 minutes.

Lemon Whippersnaps

1)   1 package lemon cake mix with pudding
2)   2 cups Cool Whip, thawed
3)   1 egg, slightly beaten
4)   1/2 cup sifted confectioners' sugar

Combine first 3 ingredients. Stir until mixture is uniformly moist. Form into small balls. Roll balls into confectioners' sugar and place on lightly greased cookie sheet. Bake in preheated oven for 10 to 12 minutes at 350 degrees.

Orange Coconut Balls

1)   3 cups finely crushed vanilla wafers
2)   2 cups flaked coconut
3)   1 cup pecans, finely chopped
4)   1 (6 ounce) can orange juice concentrate, thawed

Combine ingredients and shape into bite-sized balls. If desired, roll in crushed vanilla wafer crumbs. Refrigerate in airtight container.

Fudge Cookies

1) 1 package devil's food cake mix
2) 2 eggs
3) 1/2 cup oil
4) 1 cup semi-sweet chocolate chips

Mix cake mix, eggs and oil. Stir in chocolate chips. Mixture will be stiff. Shape dough into small balls. Place 2 inches apart on cookie sheet and bake at 350 degrees for 10 to 12 minutes.

Gold Brownies

1) 2 cups graham cracker crumbs
2) 1 (14 ounce) can sweetened condensed milk
3) 1 (6 ounce) package chocolate chips
4) 1/2 cup pecans, chopped

Mix together and place in 8x8-inch greased pan. Bake for 30 minutes at 350 degrees. Cool. Cut into squares and remove from pan.

Peanut Butter Candy Cookies

1/2 cup peanut butter
1/2 cup sugar
1/4 cup evaporated milk
2 1/2 cups cornflakes

Mix peanut butter, sugar and milk into a smooth cream. Stir in cornflakes until thoroughly blended. Drop by teaspoonful onto ungreased cookie sheet. Bake at 375 degrees for 6 minutes or until evenly browned.

Raisin Treats

1) 1/4 cup margarine
2) 1 (10 ounce) package marshmallows
3) 1 cup raisins
4) 5 cups Rice Krispies

Melt margarine over low heat in double boiler. Add marshmallows and stir until completely melted. Cook over low heat 3 minutes, stirring constantly. Remove from heat and add cereal and raisins. Stir until well coated. Pour and press mixture evenly into buttered 9x13-inch cake pan. Cut into squares when cool.

Lemon Cookies

1) 1 lemon cake mix
2) 1 stick margarine, softened
3) 1 (8 ounce) package cream cheese, softened
4) 1 egg

Mix above ingredients, blending well. Drop by teaspoonful onto lightly greased cookie sheet. Bake at 375 degrees for 10 to 12 minutes.

Cookie Tip: Let cookies cool completely before storing.
To keep cookies fresh, store soft and chewy ones
in an airtight container.
Crisp cookies in a jar with a loose fitting lid.

Chocolate Marshmallow Slices

1) 1 (12 ounce) package semi-sweet chocolate chips
2) 1/2 cup margarine
3) 6 cups (10 1/2 ounces) miniature marshmallows
4) 1 cup pecans, finely chopped

In saucepan, melt chocolate chips and margarine over low heat. Stir constantly until blended. Remove from heat, cool for 5 minutes. Stir in marshmallows and nuts. Do not melt marshmallows. On wax paper, shape mixture into 2 rolls, 2 inches in diameter. Wrap rolls in wax paper and chill overnight. Cut rolls into 1/4-inch slices. Store in airtight container until ready to serve.

Chocolate Peanut Clusters

1) 1/2 cup milk chocolate chips
2) 1/2 cup semi-sweet chocolate chips
3) 1 tablespoon shortening
4) 1 cup unsalted, roasted peanuts

Melt first 3 ingredients in double boiler, stirring until smooth. Remove from heat and stir in peanuts. Drop by teaspoonfuls into 1-inch diameter candy papers or onto wax paper. Allow to set until firm and store in airtight container.

Chocolate Bites

1) 1 (6 ounce) package semi-sweet chocolate chips
2) 1/2 cup peanut butter
3) 1/2 cup margarine
4) 8 cups Rice Chex cereal

Combine first 3 ingredients in saucepan. Cook over low heat until chips melt. Stir occasionally. Remove from heat and stir. Pour over cereal and stir to coat evenly. Spread on wax paper lined cookie sheets. Let cool 1 hour. Break into bite-size pieces.

Chocolate Truffles

1) 3/4 cup butter
2) 3/4 cup cocoa
3) 1 (14 ounce) can sweetened condensed milk
4) 1 tablespoon vanilla extract

In saucepan over low heat, melt butter, add cocoa and stir until smooth. Blend in sweetened condensed milk. Stir constantly until mixture is thick, smooth and glossy (about 4 minutes). Remove from heat and stir in vanilla. Chill 3 to 4 hours and shape into balls. Chill until firm, 1 to 2 hours. Store in refrigerator.

Toffee

1) 1 cup pecans, chopped
2) 1/4 cup packed brown sugar
3) 1/2 cup butter
4) 1/2 cup semi-sweet chocolate chips

Grease square 9x9-inch pan. Spread pecans in pan. In saucepan, heat sugar and butter to boiling point, stirring constantly. Boil over medium heat, stirring constantly, for 7 minutes. Immediately spread mixture over nuts in pan. Sprinkle chocolate chips over hot mixture. Place baking sheet over pan so contained heat will melt chocolate chips. With knife, spread the melted chocolate over candy. While hot, cut into squares. Chill.

Glazed Pecans

1) 1 egg white
2) 3/4 cup brown sugar
3) 1/2 teaspoon vanilla
4) 2 cups pecan halves

Beat egg white until soft peak will stand. Gradually add sugar and vanilla. Fold in pecans. Place pecans on greased cookie sheet, about an inch apart. Bake at 400 degrees for 30 minutes. Turn off oven and let stand in oven for another 30 minutes. Store in airtight container.

White Fudge

1)   3 tablespoons margarine
2)   3 tablespoons milk
3)   1 (15.4 ounce) package creamy white frosting mix
4)   1/2 cup chopped nuts

Butter 9x5x3-inch loaf pan. In double boiler, melt margarine in milk and stir in dry frosting mix until smooth. Heat over rapidly boiling water for 5 minutes, stirring occasionally. Stir in nuts. Spread mixture in pan. Cool until firm and then cut into squares.

Chocolate Coconut Drops

1)   2 (1 ounce) squares unsweetened chocolate
2)   1 (14 ounce) can sweetened condensed milk
3)   2 cups flaked coconut
4)   1/2 cup chopped walnuts

Preheat oven to 350 degrees. In saucepan melt chocolate over low heat. Remove from heat and stir in milk, coconut and walnuts. Drop by teaspoonfuls onto ungreased cookie sheet. Place in oven and turn off heat. Leave about 15 minutes or until candy has glazed appearance. While warm, remove from cookie sheet.

Candy Trifles

1) 1 (12 ounce) package semi-sweet chocolate chips
2) 1 cup Spanish peanuts
3) 2 cups chow mein noodles
4) 1/4 cup coconut (optional)

In double boiler over hot water, melt chocolate pieces. Stir in nuts and noodles until well coated. Add coconut if desired. Drop mixture by teaspoonfuls onto waxed paper. Chill until firm.

Carmalitas

1) 1 (18 ounce) roll refrigerated chocolate chip cookie dough
2) 32 vanilla caramels
3) 1/4 cup light cream or evaporated milk
4) 1 cup semi-sweet chocolate chips

Slice cookie dough 1/4-inch thick and place on bottom of 9x9-inch pan. Pat to make even crust. Bake at 375 degrees for 25 minutes. Cool slightly. Melt caramels and cream in double boiler. Sprinkle cookie dough with chocolate chips. Spread caramel mixture on top. Refrigerate 1 to 2 hours. Cut into squares. Makes 36 pieces.

Peanut Butter Fudge

1) 1 (10 ounce) package peanut butter chips
2) 1 (14 ounce) can sweetened condensed milk
3) 1/4 cup butter
4) 1 (6 ounce) package semi-sweet chocolate chips

Melt peanut butter chips in large saucepan. Add 1 cup sweetened condensed milk and 2 tablespoons butter. Stir. Remove from heat and spread mixture into wax paper lined 8-inch square pan. Melt chocolate chips with remaining milk and butter. Spread on top of peanut butter mixture. Chill 2 hours. Remove from refrigerator and slice.

Butterscotch Candy

1) 1 (12 ounce) package butterscotch chips
2) 1 (6 ounce) package chocolate chips
3) 2 1/2 cups chow mein noodles
4) 1/4 cup chopped pecans (optional)

Melt butterscotch and chocolate chips over double boiler. Add noodles and mix well. Pecans may be added if desired. Drop by tablespoonfuls onto waxed paper. Cool until firm.

---

*A lot of pies can be frozen, so making them
ahead saves even more time.*

Mini Chips Crescents

1) 1 (8 ounce) can refrigerated crescent rolls
2) Ground cinnamon
3) 1/2 cup semi-sweet mini-chocolate chips
4) Confectioners' sugar

Unroll crescent rolls on ungreased cookie sheet to form
8 triangles. Lightly sprinkle cinnamon and 1 tablespoon
mini-chips on top of each triangle. Gently press into dough.
Starting at short side of triangle, roll dough to opposite point.
Bake at 375 degrees for 10 to 12 minutes or until golden brown.
Sprinkle sugar over top and serve warm.

Chocolate Marshmallow Mousse

1) 1 (7 ounce) bar Hershey's milk chocolate
2) 1 1/2 cups miniature marshmallows
3) 1/3 cup milk
4) 1 cup chilled whipping cream

Break chocolate bar into pieces. In double boiler, melt chocolate
bar and marshmallows with milk. Cool to room temperature. In
small mixing bowl, beat whipping cream until stiff. Fold into
cooled chocolate mixture and pour into dessert dishes. Cover and
chill 1 to 2 hours until firm.

Mocha Mousse

1) 2 envelopes whipped topping mix
2) 3 cups cold milk
3) 1 package instant chocolate pudding mix
4) 3 tablespoons coffee

In mixing bowl, beat whipped topping with 1 cup cold milk. Add remaining milk and pudding mix. Blend well and beat for 2 minutes. Blend in coffee and pour into dessert dishes.

Caramel Popcorn Balls

1) 28 caramels
2) 2 tablespoons water
3) 2 quarts salted cooked popcorn
4) 1 teaspoon corn syrup (optional)

Melt caramels and water in double boiler. Add syrup if desired. Pour over cooked popcorn and toss until well coated. Shape into balls.

Fudge Pudding

1) 1 (3 1/2 ounce) package chocolate pudding mix
2) 2 cups milk
3) 1 cup semi-sweet chocolate chips
4) 1/4 cup pecans (optional)

In saucepan combine pudding and milk. Cook over medium heat, stirring constantly, until mixture comes to a full boil. Remove from heat and stir in chocolate chips until they are melted. Add pecans if desired. Spoon into dessert cups. Press plastic wrap directly onto surface and refrigerate until ready to serve.

Strawberry Trifle

1) 2 (3.4 ounce) packages instant vanilla pudding
2) 4 cups milk
3) 20 vanilla wafer cookies
4) 2 pints (12 ounces) strawberries, hulled and sliced

Combine pudding mix and milk and beat. Pour half of pudding into 2-quart bowl or trifle dish. Top with vanilla wafers, then sprinkle with strawberries. Top with remaining pudding. Cover and refrigerate at least 4 hours or up to 24 hours.

Apple Crisp

1) 1/3 cup butter, softened
2) 1 cup brown sugar
3) 3/4 cup flour
4) 4 cups tart apples, sliced

Mix butter, sugar and flour. Place apple slices in 8x8-inch pan. Sprinkle butter topping over apples. Bake at 350 degrees for 1 hour.

LOW FAT
&
LIGHT
FOUR
INGREDIENT
COOKBOOK

By Linda Coffee and Emily Cale

Published by Coffee and Cale

Acknowledgements

Our appreciation to Marilyn Magness RD, LD, our nutrition consultant, who had the experience and patience to calculate the nutritional breakdown of each recipe.

A big thanks to the food manufacturers that are creatively supplying an ever enlarging array of fat-free and low-fat products for us to test and taste.

And last, to a very, very special person, Emily's mother-in-law, Wilma Cale, for all her help in shopping, organizing, cooking, tasting and always being there to help us. Without her help, we would probably still be working on this book!

Special Edition   Volumes I, II, III
1998   30,000 copies

4 Ingredient Cookbook
More 4 Ingredient Cookbook
Low-Fat & Light 4 Ingredient Cookbook
1996-1998   300,000 copies

MANUFACTURED IN THE USA BY

cookbook
resources

541 Doubletree Drive
Highland Village, Texas 75067
(972) 317-0245

Special "thank you's" for their participation in cooking, testing and critiquing; their help was greatly appreciated:

1. Loma and Harold Bammel
2. Anita and Van Berson
3. Jane Maxwell and Gene Cluster
4. Chris and Dell Davis
5. Susana and Jason Dias
6. Lucy Dubuisson
7. Deda Garlitz
8. Valerie and Bill Grebe
9. Gail and Chuck Gross
10. Dawn, Hannah, Sayer, Hartley and Phil Houseal
11. Betty and Curt Johnston
12. Marilyn Magness
13. Loraine and Art Modgling
14. Patri and Brewer Newton
15. Kathy and Bill Reed
16. Mary and Rudy Rudasill
17. Virginia Stevenson

It is impossible to ignore the trend towards reducing fat in our diets. The newsstands are littered with "low-fat" articles. The grocery aisles are packed with products that are fat-free, low-fat and light.

With today's hectic lifestyles, just putting a meal on the table is a major accomplishment. Now, we are supposed to put a meal on the table and reduce the fat. If this is as challenging to you, as it is to us, these simple recipes are sure to be helpful.

Marilyn Schad Magness RD,LD

Marilyn was born in Tulsa, Oklahoma and graduated from the University of Oklahoma in Norman and then completed her Dietetic Internship at the OU Health Sciences in Oklahoma City. Following completion of the internship in 1973, she became a Registered Dietitian and worked as a Nutrition Consultant for the Dairy Council in San Antonio and Houston and as a Program Coordinator in Memphis. After having three children, Marilyn worked as a Consulting Dietitian to health care facilities and she is currently employed as a Clinical Dietitian at the South Texas Veterans Health Care System in Kerrville. She also consulted part time at Ultrafit Preventive Medicine facilities teaching nutrition and low-fat cooking classes.

The children are now teenagers and they are learning to help with the cooking. Marilyn says, *"The Four Ingredient Cookbooks are even more simple to use than some of the children's recipe books I've bought at times to encourage my children to explore cooking. My parents always encouraged me to help in the kitchen and I grew to love cooking. Like many other working parents, I just don't have time to prepare long involved recipes. I think this series of cookbooks is very timely and I am glad to be a part of the Low Fat & Light Four Ingredient Cookbook."*

Please note the following about the analysis of the recipes in the *Low Fat & Light Four Ingredient Cookbook*:

The analysis for the cookbook was done using the Professional Nutritionist computer software program which includes the USDA database of foods and an All Foods database. Additional foods were added to the database by using manufacturer's food labels.

Recipes calling for chicken breasts were analyzed using Individually Quick Frozen (IQF) chicken breasts.

Recipes using marinades or sauces include the full amount of the ingredients listed.

Recipes may be further modified to decrease sodium by omitting salt from the recipe or by using unsalted products when available.

Recipe analysis is an approximation and different results may be obtained by using different nutrient databases. Manufacturers' nutrition labels may also change from time to time.

We have listed a few helpful ingredients that are good to keep on hand in learning to cook and eat a low-fat diet!

Fat Free Margarine	Skim Milk
Fat Free Cream Cheese	Liquid Egg Substitute
Fat Free Salad Dressings	Salsas
Fat Free Sour Cream	Mustard
Fat Free Ice Cream	Selection of Grains
Fat Free Yogurt	Rice Cakes
Fat Free Frozen Yogurt	Hot Pepper Sauce
Fat Free Soups	Flavored Tomato Sauces
Fat Free Mayonnaise	BBQ Sauce
Fat Free Lunch Meats	Non-fat Refried Beans
Fat Free Hot Dogs	Flavored Vinegars
Fat Free Crackers	Pretzels
Fat Free Sweetened	Fruits
Condensed Milk	Vegetables
Fat Free Gravies	Plain Popcorn
Fat Free Flour Tortillas	Dried Mushrooms
Fat Free Brownies	Tuna Packed in Water
Fat Free Cookies	Beans
Pastas in Different Shapes	Dried and Fresh Herbs and
and Flavors	Spices

Table of Contents

Appetizers **11**

Salads **27**

Vegetables **42**

Main Dishes **65**

Desserts **109**

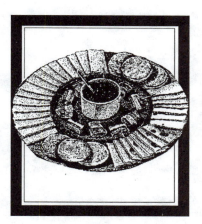

Appetizers

Tangy Dip

1)   1 cup fat-free sour cream
2)   2 tablespoons chili sauce
3)   2 teaspoons prepared horseradish
4)   Fresh vegetables

Mix above ingredients. Cover and refrigerate at least 1 hour. Serve with fresh vegetables.

Per Tablespoon:

Calories	8.43	Protein	1.37g
Total Fat	0g	Carbohydrate	0.80g
Saturated Fat	0g	Cholesterol	0mg
Sodium	25.85mg	Fiber	0g

Curry Dip

1)   1 cup fat-free sour cream
2)   1 teaspoon curry powder
3)   1/2 teaspoon lemon juice
4)   1/2 teaspoon ground cumin

Combine above ingredients and chill. Serve with fresh vegetables.

Per Tablespoon:

Calories	8.04	Protein	1.54g
Total Fat	0.02g	Carbohydrate	0.59g
Saturated Fat	0g	Cholesterol	0mg
Sodium	7.66mg	Fiber	0.04g

Chili con Queso

1) 2 pounds fat-free cheddar cheese, grated
2) 1 (10 ounce) can Rotel tomatoes and green chilies
3) Fat-free chips
4) Fresh vegetables or fat free tortilla chips

Melt cheese slowly in saucepan or microwave. Stir in tomatoes. Use as a dip with fat-free tortilla chips or vegetables.

Per Tablespoon (Dip Only):

Calories	16.33	Protein	3.54g
Total Fat	0g	Carbohydrate	0.52g
Saturated Fat	0g	Cholesterol	0mg
Sodium	13.87mg	Fiber	0g

California Dip

1) 2 cups fat-free cottage cheese
2) 1 tablespoon lemon juice
3) 2 tablespoons skim milk
4) 1 envelope onion soup mix

Mix cottage cheese and lemon juice in blender. Add skim milk. Place in bowl and stir in onion soup mix. Chill before serving with fresh vegetables.

Per Tablespoon:

Calories	10.11	Protein	1.50g
Total Fat	0.10g	Carbohydrate	0.78g
Saturated Fat	0.04g	Cholesterol	0.59mg
Sodium	95.75mg	Fiber	0.11g

Chile Salsa

1) 1 cup chopped seeded tomatoes
2) 1/2 cup chopped green onions
3) 1 (4 ounce) can diced green chilies
4) Fat-free tortilla chips

Mix above ingredients together and refrigerate. Serve with fat-free tortilla chips.

Per Tablespoon (Dip Only):

Calories	2.55	Protein	0.11g
Total Fat	0.02g	Carbohydrate	0.59g
Saturated Fat	0g	Cholesterol	0mg
Sodium	42.31mg	Fiber	0.17g

Light Guacamole

1) 1 (20 ounce) bag frozen peas, defrosted
2) 1/4 cup fresh lime juice
3) 1/2 bunch of green onions, diced
4) 1/4 cup picante sauce

In blender, blend peas, lime juice and onions. Remove to mixing bowl and mix in picante sauce. Refrigerate until ready to serve. Serve with fat-free tortilla chips.

Per Tablespoon:

Calories	9.29	Protein	0.56g
Total Fat	0.03g	Carbohydrate	1.80g
Saturated Fat	0g	Cholesterol	0mg
Sodium	13.82mg	Fiber	0.62g

Almond Fruit Dip

1) 2 cups (16 ounces) low-fat cottage cheese
2) 1/2 cup confectioners' sugar
3) 1 (4 ounce) package fat-free cream cheese
4) 1 teaspoon almond extract

In blender, add above ingredients and blend until smooth. Cover and chill until ready to serve. Serve with fresh fruit.

Per Tablespoon:

Calories	16.58	Protein	1.71g
Total Fat	0.11g	Carbohydrate	2.10g
Saturated Fat	0.07g	Cholesterol	0.48mg
Sodium	57.82mg	Fiber	0g

Apple Curry Dip

1) 1 1/2 cups low-fat cottage cheese
2) 1 cup unsweetened applesauce
3) 1 envelope onion soup mix
4) 2 teaspoons curry powder

In blender, blend cottage cheese and applesauce until smooth. Stir in soup mix and curry powder. Serve with raw vegetables.

Per Tablespoon:

Calories	11.97	Protein	1.19g
Total Fat	0.16g	Carbohydrate	1.50g
Saturated Fat	0.07g	Cholesterol	0.42mg
Sodium	122.0mg	Fiber	0.21g

Roquefort Dip

1) 1/2 cup crumbled Roquefort or bleu cheese
2) 2 cups (16 ounces) low-fat cottage cheese
3) 1 teaspoon dried onion flakes
4) Pepper, to taste

Combine and blend above ingredients. Chill until ready to serve. Serve with vegetables.

Per Tablespoon:

Calories	18.67	Protein	2.02g
Total Fat	0.98g	Carbohydrate	0.37g
Saturated Fat	0.62g	Cholesterol	3.05mg
Sodium	97.32mg	Fiber	0g

Spanish Olive Spread

1) 1 (8 ounce) carton fat-free sour cream
2) 1/4 cup green pimiento stuffed olives, chopped
3) 1/4 cup liquid from olive jar
4) Paprika

In blender place sour cream and olive liquid and blend until smooth. Pour into bowl and add olives. Mix thoroughly. Sprinkle with paprika and refrigerate. Serve as a spread on party rye bread.

Per Tablespoon:

Calories	7.15	Protein	1.01g
Total Fat	0.21g	Carbohydrate	0.42g
Saturated Fat	0g	Cholesterol	0mg
Sodium	28.42mg	Fiber	0g

Fruited Cheese Spread

1)   1 (8 ounce) package fat-free cream cheese, room
            temperature
2)   1 tablespoon concentrated orange juice, defrosted
3)   Few drops vanilla extract
4)   Toast rounds

Combine above ingredients and mix well. Spread on toast rounds
or slices of high fiber bread cut in fourths.

Per Tablespoon (Spread Only):

Calories	15.86	Protein	1.74g
Total Fat	0g	Carbohydrate	2.03g
Saturated Fat	0g	Cholesterol	0mg
Sodium	63.56	Fiber	0.02g

Pimiento Cream Spread

1)   2 cups low-fat cottage cheese
2)   1 teaspoon onion powder
3)   1 (3 ounce) jar pimientos, drained
4)   Celery

Mix above ingredients in blender. Serve as a spread or stuff celery
stalks.

Per Tablespoon (Spread Only):

Calories	9.35	Protein	1.49g
Total Fat	0.13g	Carbohydrate	0.51g
Saturated Fat	0.08g	Cholesterol	0.52mg
Sodium	47.95mg	Fiber	0.03g

Pimiento Cheese Spread

1) 1 pound fat-free cheese, cubed
2) 1 (3 ounce) jar pimientos, drained
3) 1/2 cup fat-free mayonnaise
4) Crackers or fresh vegetables

Blend above ingredients until smooth. Spread on crackers or vegetables.

Per Tablespoon (Spread Only):

Calories	16.24	Protein	3.14g
Total Fat	0g	Carbohydrate	0.88g
Saturated Fat	0g	Cholesterol	0mg
Sodium	29.30mg	Fiber	0g

Tropical Cheese Spread

1) 1/2 cup fat-free cottage cheese
2) 1/4 cup crushed pineapple, drained
3) 1 teaspoon lemon juice
4) Cocktail rye bread or crackers

Combine first three ingredients and mix in blender until smooth. Serve on cocktail rye bread or crackers.

Per Tablespoon (Spread Only):

Calories	11.01	Protein	1.63g
Total Fat	0.04g	Carbohydrate	0.92g
Saturated Fat	0.03g	Cholesterol	0.63mg
Sodium	1.63mg	Fiber	0.04g

Bagel Chips

1) 1 low-fat bagel (try assorted flavors)
2) Non-fat butter spray
3) 1/8 teaspoon garlic powder
4) 1/8 teaspoon Cajun seasoning

Slice bagel into 1/4-inch thick rounds. Place in microwave bowl and cook on high for 1 minute. Gently stir. Continue to microwave in 1 minute increments, stirring after each minute, approximately 3 minutes. Watch carefully. Chips should be crisp. (If over-microwaved char spots will appear.) Remove from microwave and spray with butter spray and sprinkle with garlic powder and Cajun seasoning. Makes great chips for dips and spreads. 2 Servings

Per Serving:

Calories	135.0	Protein	4.00g
Total Fat	0.25g	Carbohydrate	29.00g
Saturated Fat	0g	Cholesterol	0mg
Sodium	283.4mg	Fiber	1.50g

Potato Skins

1) 4 potatoes, baked
2) 8 ounces reduced fat cheddar cheese, grated
3) 1 cup fat-free sour cream
4) 2 tablespoons chopped green onion

Cut each potato into quarters lengthwise. Scoop out pulp. Spray
potato skins with cooking spray and place on baking pan. Bake
at 425 degrees for 10 minutes. Turn and bake for an additional
5 to 8 minutes or until crisp and light brown. Remove from oven
and place cheese, sour cream and onions on each quarter. Return
to oven and bake until cheese melts.

Per Quarter:

Calories	105.3	Protein	6.78g
Total Fat	2.53g	Carbohydrate	14.42g
Saturated Fat	0g	Cholesterol	10.00mg
Sodium	83.80mg	Fiber	1.18g

Sherried Meat Balls

1)   2 pounds lean ground beef
2)   1 cup catsup
3)   1 cup cooking sherry
4)   2 tablespoons brown sugar

Heat oven to 350 degrees. Season ground beef to taste and shape into 1-inch meat balls. Place meat balls in oven for 30 minutes to brown. Remove meat balls from browning pan and place into a casserole. Mix remaining three ingredients and pour over meat balls. Bake an additional 30 minutes. Serve meat balls with sauce. 50 meat balls.

Per Meat Ball:

Calories	61.42	Protein	4.57g
Total Fat	3.37g	Carbohydrate	1.85g
Saturated Fat	1.32g	Cholesterol	15.79mg
Sodium	71.45mg	Fiber	0.06g

Mexican Meat Balls

1)   1 pound lean ground beef
2)   1 package taco seasoning mix
3)   Salsa
4)   Salt and pepper to taste (optional)

Mix lean ground beef and taco seasoning and shape into 1-inch meat balls. Season further with salt and pepper if desired. Brown in skillet and place on paper towel to drain. Reheat in oven and serve with chilled salsa. 25 meat balls.

Per Meat Ball:

Calories	57.17	Protein	4.58g
Total Fat	3.33g	Carbohydrate	1.90g
Saturated Fat	1.31g	Cholesterol	14.15mg
Sodium	129.4mg	Fiber	0g

Party Drummettes

1) 2 pounds chicken drummettes, skin removed
2) 1/4 cup low-sodium soy sauce
3) 1/4 cup wine vinegar
4) 1/4 teaspoon garlic powder

Broil drummettes, 8 minutes one side; turn and broil 6 minutes on other side until browned. Combine drummettes with remaining ingredients in a shallow baking dish. Cover and bake at 350 degrees for 30 minutes or until tender. Makes 20 drummettes.

Per Drummette:

Calories	80.46	Protein	13.02g
Total Fat	2.57g	Carbohydrate	0.51g
Saturated Fat	0.67g	Cholesterol	42.18mg
Sodium	248.9mg	Fiber	0g

Pizza Sticks

1) 1 can refrigerated Pillsbury pizza crust
2) Non-fat butter spray
3) 1/2 teaspoon garlic powder
4) 1/2 teaspoon parsley flakes

Unroll pizza dough and place in shallow baking pan. Spray both sides with butter spray. Sprinkle with garlic and parsley. Cut into 8 long strips. Bake at 425 degrees for 10 to 15 minutes. Turn strips over and bake additional 5 to 7 minutes. 4 Servings.

Per Serving:

Calories	180.6	Protein	6.03g
Total Fat	2.50g	Carbohydrate	33.13g
Saturated Fat	0.50g	Cholesterol	0mg
Sodium	390.1mg	Fiber	1.00g

Mini Heroes

1) 1 container Pillsbury dinner rolls
2) 2 tablespoons Dijon mustard
3) 1 (6 ounce) package Healthy Choice smoked ham
4) 1/2 cup Healthy Choice non-fat pizza cheese

Place rolls on sprayed baking sheet. Stretch rolls to form a 4-inch circle. Combine mustard, ham and cheese. Place mixture in center of roll, dividing equally. Fold roll over in center and seal by pressing edge with a fork. Bake at 375 degrees for 15 to 18 minutes. 8 Servings.

Per Serving:

Calories	147.5	Protein	10.63g
Total Fat	2.56g	Carbohydrate	18.88g
Saturated Fat	0.19g	Cholesterol	10.63mg
Sodium	586.3mg	Fiber	1.00g

Green Chili Pie

1) 1 (4.5 ounce) can green chilies, diced
2) 2 cups Healthy Choice non-fat pizza cheese
3) 1 (4 ounce) container Egg Beaters (equals 2 eggs)
4) 2 green onions, chopped

Place green chilies in a 7 1/2x11 1/2-inch ovenproof casserole. Sprinkle with cheese and onions. Pour eggs over top. Sprinkle with paprika for garnish. Bake at 350 degrees for 10 to 15 minutes. 15 servings.

Per Serving:

Calories	30.36	Protein	5.78g
Total Fat	0g	Carbohydrate	1.52g
Saturated Fat	0g	Cholesterol	2.68mg
Sodium	155.2mg	Fiber	0.32g

Salmon Pinwheels

1) 6 fat-free flour tortillas
2) 1 (6 ounce) container salmon flavored fat-free cream cheese
3) 1/2 cup salmon, flaked, bones and skin removed
4) 2 green onions, chopped

Combine cream cheese, salmon and onions. Spread each tortilla with mixture and roll. Place in airtight container and refrigerate. Before serving, remove and slice across tortilla every inch. Makes 36 pinwheels — 2 per serving.

Per Serving:

Calories	46.70	Protein	3.95g
Total Fat	0.56g	Carbohydrate	6.38g
Saturated Fat	0.11g	Cholesterol	6.07mg
Sodium	180.5mg	Fiber	0.02g

Salads

Apple Coleslaw

1)   2 cups cabbage, shredded
2)   2 medium apples, cored and diced
3)   1 (16 ounce) can crushed pineapple, drained
4)   3/4 cup fat-free mayonnaise

Combine above ingredients, cover and refrigerate 1 hour or more before serving. 8 Servings.

Per Serving:

Calories	60.87	Protein	0.56g
Total Fat	0.22g	Carbohydrate	15.42g
Saturated Fat	0.03g	Cholesterol	0mg
Sodium	288.7mg	Fiber	1.7g

Apple Salad with Feta Cheese

1)   1 large head bibb lettuce, torn in bite-sized pieces
2)   1 large red delicious apple, diced
3)   2 ounces Feta cheese, crumbled
4)   1/4 cup Pritikin fat-free raspberry vinaigrette

Dice apples right before serving and toss with raspberry vinaigrette. Combine with other ingredients. 4 Servings.

Per Serving:

Calories	82.01	Protein	2.21g
Total Fat	3.17g	Carbohydrate	11.69g
Saturated Fat	2.14g	Cholesterol	12.62mg
Sodium	194.1mg	Fiber	1.12g

Beet and Onion Salad

1)   1/4 cup wine vinegar
2)   1 teaspoon sugar
3)   1 (16 ounce) can sliced beets, undrained
4)   1/2 onion, sliced in rings

Combine above ingredients and marinate at room temperature at least 30 minutes before serving. Stir every 10 minutes. 8 Servings.

Per Serving:

Calories	24.36	Protein	0.63g
Total Fat	0.10g	Carbohydrate	5.89g
Saturated Fat	0.02g	Cholesterol	0mg
Sodium	155.7mg	Fiber	1.20g

Broccoli Salad

1)   1 bunch fresh broccoli spears
2)   2 ounces Feta cheese
3)   1/2 head lettuce, torn in bite-sized pieces
4)   1/2 cup fat-free salad dressing

Combine above ingredients and serve. 6 Servings.

Per Serving:

Calories	60.90	Protein	3.72g
Total Fat	2.29g	Carbohydrate	7.26g
Saturated Fat	1.45g	Cholesterol	8.38mg
Sodium	292.6mg	Fiber	0.19g

Carrot Raisin Celery Salad

1) 6 cups grated carrots
2) 1 cup raisins
3) 2 cups sliced celery
4) 1/3 cup fat-free mayonnaise

Mix above ingredients and chill at least 1 hour. 8 Servings.

Per Serving:

Calories	101.3	Protein	1.66g
Total Fat	0.28g	Carbohydrate	25.12g
Saturated Fat	0.06g	Cholesterol	0mg
Sodium	139.7mg	Fiber	3.71g

Marinated Cauliflower Salad

1) 1 head cauliflower, divided into flowerets and thinly sliced
2) 1 small onion, thinly sliced
3) 12 small pimiento stuffed olives, sliced
4) 1/3 cup Kraft fat-free Catalina salad dressing

Mix all ingredients, cover and refrigerate at least 1 hour before serving. Stir occasionally. 8 Servings.

Per Serving:

Calories	33.11	Protein	1.11g
Total Fat	0.75g	Carbohydrate	5.69g
Saturated Fat	0.02g	Cholesterol	0mg
Sodium	164.5mg	Fiber	1.43g

Cucumber Salad

1) 1/4 cup white vinegar
2) 1 tablespoon honey
3) 1/2 medium green pepper, diced
4) 4 medium cucumbers, peeled and thinly sliced

Combine vinegar and honey and pour over cucumbers and green peppers. Chill for several hours before serving. 8 Servings.

Per Serving:
Calories	17.48	Protein	0.42g
Total Fat	0.08g	Carbohydrate	4.44g
Saturated Fat	0.02g	Cholesterol	0mg
Sodium	1.35mg	Fiber	0.53g

Cucumber Strawberry Salad

1) 1/4 cup fresh lime juice
2) 1 small green pepper, diced
3) 1 cucumber, peeled and sliced
4) 2 cups fresh or frozen strawberries, quartered

Combine lime juice and pepper. Toss mixture with cucumbers and strawberries. Chill before serving. 4 Servings.

Per Serving:
Calories	34.88	Protein	0.87g
Total Fat	0.36g	Carbohydrate	8.52g
Saturated Fat	0.03g	Cholesterol	0mg
Sodium	1.79mg	Fiber	2.32g

Sweet and Sour Cucumber Salad

1) 2 medium cucumbers, peeled and sliced
2) 1 teaspoon salt
3) 1 tablespoon vinegar
4) 3 tablespoons sugar

Place sliced cucumbers in bowl and mix well with salt. Let stand 15 minutes. Drain off all the salty fluid. Add vinegar and sugar and let stand 10 minutes. Before serving, drain sweet and sour juice from cucumber slices and place cucumbers into a serving bowl. 4 Servings.

Per Serving:

Calories	42.11	Protein	0.36g
Total Fat	0.07g	Carbohydrate	10.65g
Saturated Fat	0.02g	Cholesterol	0mg
Sodium	582.5mg	Fiber	0.42g

Fruit Salad

1) 1(20 ounce) can pineapple chunks, drained
2) 2 (11 ounce) cans mandarin oranges, drained
3) 1 cup miniature marshmallows
4) 1/3 cup fat-free mayonnaise

Toss together above ingredients and refrigerate. 6 Servings.

Per Serving:

Calories	125.6	Protein	0.80g
Total Fat	0.02g	Carbohydrate	31.11g
Saturated Fat	0g	Cholesterol	0mg
Sodium	133.6mg	Fiber	1.33g

Medley of Fruit

1) 1 (26 ounce) jar mango wedges, drained and chopped
2) 2 medium kiwi fruits, pared and thinly sliced
3) 2 medium bananas, thinly sliced
4) 1 teaspoon lemon juice

Toss above ingredients in lemon juice and chill. 8 Servings.

Per Serving:

Calories	119.2	Protein	0.48g
Total Fat	0.63g	Carbohydrate	29.87g
Saturated Fat	0.05g	Cholesterol	0mg
Sodium	5.30mg	Fiber	1.33g

Green Bean and Baby Corn Salad

1) 1 pound green beans, trimmed
2) 1 (7 ounce) can pickled baby ears of corn, undrained
3) Juice from corn
4) 4 green onions, sliced

Blanch beans for 5 to 6 minutes in salted water until crisp tender. Drain, rinse and cool. Combine with baby corn and onions. Juice from corn acts as dressing. Toss and chill. 6 Servings.

Per Serving:

Calories	36.35	Protein	2.68g
Total Fat	0.11g	Carbohydrate	7.12g
Saturated Fat	0.02g	Cholesterol	0mg
Sodium	110.4mg	Fiber	3.93g

Hearts of Palm Salad

1) 2 heads Boston lettuce, torn in bite-sized pieces
2) 6 green onions, sliced
3) 1 (14 ounce) can hearts of palm, drained and sliced
   horizontally
4) 1/2 cup low-fat vinaigrette dressing

Toss lettuce, onions and hearts of palm. Pour vinaigrette dressing over salad and serve. 6 Servings.

Per Serving:

Calories	36.27	Protein	1.41
Total Fat	1.93g	Carbohydrate	3.73g
Saturated Fat	0.26g	Cholesterol	1.15mg
Sodium	387.7mg	Fiber	1.56g

Snow Pea Salad

1) 2 cups snow peas, trimmed
2) 1 red bell pepper, sliced
3) 1 teaspoon toasted sesame seeds
4) 1/2 cup Hidden Valley fat-free Italian Parmesan salad
   dressing

Blanch the snow peas and drain, running under cold water. Pat dry and refrigerate for an hour. When ready to serve, place snow peas in a circle on individual plates. Arrange red pepper strips between snow peas and sprinkle with sesame seeds. Drizzle salad dressing over top of each salad. 4 Servings.

Per Serving:

Calories	63.68	Protein	2.44g
Total Fat	0.76g	Carbohydrate	11.36g
Saturated Fat	0.11g	Cholesterol	0mg
Sodium	243.5mg	Fiber	2.54g

Bell Pepper Salad

1) 1 medium red bell pepper, sliced
2) 1 medium green bell pepper, sliced
3) 1 medium yellow bell pepper, sliced
4) 1/4 cup fat-free vinaigrette dressing

Mix peppers in large bowl and toss with dressing. Refrigerate until ready to serve. 6 servings.

Per Serving:

Calories	30.42	Protein	1.06g
Total Fat	0.22g	Carbohydrate	7.16g
Saturated Fat	0.01g	Cholesterol	0mg
Sodium	10.23mg	Fiber	0.94g

Hearty Spinach and Mushroom Salad

1) 1 (10 ounce) bag cold water washed spinach, torn in bite-sized pieces
2) 1 (8 ounce) package sliced mushrooms
3) 1 medium zucchini, sliced
4) 1/2 cup fat-free red wine vinegar dressing

In large bowl, toss spinach, mushrooms and zucchini. Add dressing and toss again. 8 Servings.

Per Serving:

Calories	39.66	Protein	1.79g
Total Fat	0.27g	Carbohydrate	8.53g
Saturated Fat	0.04g	Cholesterol	0mg
Sodium	64.62mg	Fiber	1.49g

Sunshine Salad

1) 1 (10 ounce) package cold water washed spinach, torn in bite-sized pieces
2) 2 navel oranges, peeled, sectioned and cut in half
3) 1/2 thinly sliced red onion
4) 1/2 cup fat-free fruited salad dressing (Paul's No Oil Tangerine and Mint Dressing)

Mix spinach, oranges and red onion. Toss with dressing and chill until ready to serve. 8 Servings.

Per Serving:

Calories	31.99	Protein	1.44g
Total Fat	0.18g	Carbohydrate	6.95g
Saturated Fat	0.03g	Cholesterol	0mg
Sodium	40.30mg	Fiber	1.92g

Tangy Spinach Salad

1) 1 (10 ounce) package cold water washed spinach, torn in bite-sized pieces
2) 1 cup low-fat cottage cheese
3) 1 red bell pepper, thinly sliced
4) 1/2 cup fat-free honey mustard salad dressing

Combine above ingredients and toss with dressing. 8 Servings.

Per Serving:

Calories	55.74	Protein	5.18g
Total Fat	0.45g	Carbohydrate	8.20g
Saturated Fat	0.21g	Cholesterol	1.24mg
Sodium	238.1mg	Fiber	1.33g

Spinach with Sprouts

1) 1 (10 ounce) package cold water washed spinach, torn in bite-size pieces
2) 2 cups fresh bean sprouts
3) 1 (8 1/2 ounce) can water chestnuts, sliced and drained
4) 1/2 cup fat-free mayonnaise

Mix above ingredients and serve. 8 Servings.

Per Serving:

Calories	40.66	Protein	2.07g
Total Fat	0.19g	Carbohydrate	8.53g
Saturated Fat	0.03g	Cholesterol	0mg
Sodium	157.1mg	Fiber	1.42g

Fruit and Spinach Salad

1) 1 (10 ounce) package cold water washed spinach, torn in bite-sized pieces
2) 1 large red delicious apple, cored and chopped
3) 1 medium pear, cored and chopped
4) 4 green onions, sliced

Combine above ingredients and toss with a fruited fat-free vinaigrette dressing. 8 Servings.

Per Serving:

Calories	54.64	Protein	1.24g
Total Fat	0.28g	Carbohydrate	12.95g
Saturated Fat	0.04g	Cholesterol	0mg
Sodium	63.96mg	Fiber	2.08g

Spinach Chicken Salad

1)   2 (10 ounce) packages frozen chopped spinach
2)   1 pound chicken breasts (cooked, skinless, boneless)
3)   2 tablespoons lemon pepper
4)   1 cup fat-free mayonnaise

Thaw spinach and pat dry with paper towel. Place in large bowl. Shred chicken breasts and add to spinach. Toss spinach and chicken with lemon pepper and mayonnaise. 6 Servings.

Per Serving:

Calories	172.5	Protein	26.21g
Total Fat	3.04g	Carbohydrate	8.66g
Saturated Fat	0.82g	Cholesterol	64.39mg
Sodium	464.9mg	Fiber	2.56g

Sweet Potato Salad

1)   3 (1/2 pound) sweet potatoes
2)   1 medium onion, sliced into thin rings
3)   1 green pepper, cut into thin strips
4)   1/4 cup fat-free vinaigrette dressing

Heat enough water to boiling to cover sweet potatoes. Add sweet potatoes and return to boil. Cover and cook 30 minutes or just until fork tender. Do not overcook. Cool and slice into 1/4-inch slices. Combine sweet potato slices, onion rings and green pepper strips in large bowl. Refrigerate at least one hour. Toss lightly with vinaigrette dressing. 8 Servings.

Per Serving:

Calories	105.5	Protein	1.80g
Total Fat	0.32g	Carbohydrate	24.29g
Saturated Fat	0.06g	Cholesterol	0mg
Sodium	108.0mg	Fiber	2.82g

Romaine Strawberry Salad

1) 1 head Romaine lettuce, torn into bite-size pieces
2) 1 cup fresh strawberries, sliced
3) 1/2 purple onion, coarsely chopped
4) 1/4 cup Pritikin raspberry vinaigrette dressing

Combine first three ingredients and toss gently. Serve with
raspberry vinaigrette salad dressing. 6 Servings.

Per Serving:

Calories	29.17	Protein	0.47g
Total Fat	0.13g	Carbohydrate	6.81g
Saturated Fat	0.01g	Cholesterol	0mg
Sodium	24.83mg	Fiber	1.05g

Italian Tomato Cheese Salad

1) 12 cherry tomatoes, cut in halves
2) 1 ounce mozzarella cheese, cut in cubes
3) 4 pitted black olives, sliced
4) 1 tablespoon fat-free Italian salad dressing

Mix above ingredients and toss lightly to coat with dressing.
Refrigerate until chilled. Serve on a bed of lettuce. 4 Servings.

Per Serving:

Calories	52.21	Protein	2.82g
Total Fat	2.59g	Carbohydrate	5.38g
Saturated Fat	0.95g	Cholesterol	3.83mg
Sodium	185.4	Fiber	1.01g

Turkey Salad

1)   3 cups cooked cubed turkey breasts
2)   1 (16 ounce) can pineapple tidbits, drained
3)   1 (8 ounce) can sliced water chestnuts, drained
4)   4 green onions, sliced

Combine above ingredients and serve with a fat-free honey mustard dressing. 6 Servings.

Per Serving:

Calories	161.8	Protein	22.53g
Total Fat	0.04g	Carbohydrate	17.32g
Saturated Fat	0g	Cholesterol	501.0mg
Sodium	946.4mg	Fiber	0.88g

Luncheon Tuna Salad

1)   1 (10 ounce) can water-packed tuna, drained
2)   1 (8 ounce) can peas, drained
3)   3/4 cup finely chopped celery
4)   1/2 cup fat-free mayonnaise

Toss all ingredients and chill. Serve on a bed of lettuce. 4 Servings.

Per Serving:

Calories	159.1	Protein	21.57g
Total Fat	1.97g	Carbohydrate	11.95g
Saturated Fat	0.51g	Cholesterol	29.77mg
Sodium	671.6mg	Fiber	2.71g

Marinated Vegetable Salad

1)   **2 cups cauliflower pieces**
2)   **2 cups broccoli pieces**
3)   **1 basket cherry tomatoes, cut in halves**
4)   **1 (8 ounce) bottle fat-free Italian dressing**

Mix above ingredients and chill overnight. 6 Servings.

Per Serving:

Calories	43.64	Protein	2.02g
Total Fat	0.36g	Carbohydrate	8.43g
Saturated Fat	0.05g	Cholesterol	0mg
Sodium	553.3mg	Fiber	1.46g

_____

*Most fresh and frozen fruits and vegetables are
naturally low in fat and calories and high in
vitamins and minerals. Combine them with
dressings and condiments that are low in fat or fat
free and you can eat all you want.*

Vegetables

Tarragon Asparagus

1) 1 pound fresh asparagus spears
2) Non-fat butter spray
3) 1 tablespoon tarragon
4) 1/4 teaspoon pepper

Wash asparagus and break off at tender point. Steam over boiling water for 6 minutes or until barely tender. Remove from heat and drain. Spray with butter spray and sprinkle with tarragon and pepper. 4 Servings.

Per Serving:

Calories	26.08	Protein	2.59g
Total Fat	0.23g	Carbohydrate	5.15g
Saturated Fat	0.05g	Cholesterol	0mg
Sodium	2.27mg	Fiber	2.38g

Asparagus with Sesame Seeds

1) 1 pound fresh asparagus spears
2) 2 tablespoons lime juice
3) 1 tablespoon sesame seeds
4) Pimiento strips, for garnish

Wash asparagus and break off at tender point. In large saucepan bring 1/2 cup water to a boil and add asparagus. Cover and steam until just tender, around 6 minutes. Remove from heat and drain. Place on platter, decorate with pimiento strips and sprinkle with lime juice and sesame seeds. Serve warm or cold. 4 Servings.

Per Serving:

Calories	41.83	Protein	3.21g
Total Fat	1.33g	Carbohydrate	6.44g
Saturated Fat	0.21g	Cholesterol	0mg
Sodium	3.14mg	Fiber	2.41g

Dijon Broccoli

1) 1 cup (about 4 ounces) uncooked pasta
2) 1 (10 ounce) package frozen chopped broccoli, cooked and
   drained
3) 1/4 cup low-fat sour cream
4) 2 tablespoons Dijon mustard

Cook pasta according to package directions. Drain. Combine
broccoli, sour cream and mustard with pasta. Toss all ingredients
until well mixed. Chill until ready to serve. 4 Servings.

Per Serving:

Calories	125.5	Protein	5.88g
Total Fat	1.68g	Carbohydrate	20.25g
Saturated Fat	0.11g	Cholesterol	25.42mg
Sodium	213.8mg	Fiber	2.13g

Parmesan Broccoli and Mushrooms

1) 1 (10 ounce) package frozen chopped broccoli, cooked and
   drained
2) 1 (4 1/2 ounce) jar sliced mushrooms, drained
3) 2 tablespoons fat-free margarine
4) 1/4 cup grated Parmesan cheese

While broccoli is still warm, combine above ingredients. Toss and
serve. 4 Servings.

Per Serving:

Calories	51.37	Protein	4.67g
Total Fat	1.80g	Carbohydrate	5.16g
Saturated Fat	1.00g	Cholesterol	3.93mg
Sodium	290.6mg	Fiber	2.89g

Lemon Brussels Sprouts

1) 1 (10 ounce) package frozen brussels sprouts
2) 1/4 cup fat-free margarine
3) 2 teaspoons chopped parsley
4) 2 teaspoons grated lemon rind

Prepare brussels sprouts according to package directions. Drain and place in serving bowl. In small saucepan, melt margarine and stir in parsley and lemon rind. Heat and pour over sprouts.
4 Servings.

Per Serving:

Calories	34.95	Protein	2.70g
Total Fat	0.29g	Carbohydrate	5.61g
Saturated Fat	0.06g	Cholesterol	0.06mg
Sodium	97.35mg	Fiber	2.69g

Minted Carrots

1) 3 cups sliced carrots
2) 1 tablespoon honey
3) 1 teaspoon fresh or dried mint leaves
4) Butter spray

Heat 1-inch water to boiling and add carrots. When water returns to boiling, reduce heat and cover. Cook carrots until crisp-tender, around 10 minutes. Drain and toss with honey, mint and butter spray. 4 Servings.

Per Serving:

Calories	53.40	Protein	1.06g
Total Fat	0.20g	Carbohydrate	12.96g
Saturated Fat	0.04g	Cholesterol	0mg
Sodium	56.85mg	Fiber	3.08g

Honey Carrots

1) 4 cups baby carrots
2) 2 tablespoons firmly packed brown sugar
3) 2 tablespoons honey
4) 2 tablespoons fat-free margarine

Combine brown sugar, margarine and honey in saucepan and stir until melted. Place carrots in ovenproof casserole with cover. Pour honey mixture over carrots and toss. Bake at 400 degrees for 1 hour. Stir occasionally to coat carrots with honey mixture. 8 Servings.

Per Serving:

Calories	54.09	Protein	0.64g
Total Fat	0.40g	Carbohydrate	12.62g
Saturated Fat	0.07g	Cholesterol	0mg
Sodium	49.71mg	Fiber	22.40g

Ginger Carrots

1) 1 pound package mini-carrots
2) 1 teaspoon brown sugar
3) 1 teaspoon fat-free margarine
4) 1/8 teaspoon ground ginger

Place carrots in steam rack over boiling water and steam around 10 minutes. Remove from heat and set aside. In saucepan, melt margarine and add brown sugar and ginger. Cook over low heat, stirring constantly, until sugar is dissolved. Add carrots and stir gently until carrots are well coated and heated thoroughly. 4 Servings.

Per Serving:

Calories	46.35	Protein	0.95g
Total Fat	0.60g	Carbohydrate	9.99g
Saturated Fat	0.10g	Cholesterol	0mg
Sodium	47.48mg	Fiber	0g

Carrots and Zucchini

1) 3 medium carrots, peeled and sliced
2) 1 medium zucchini, sliced
3) 1/2 cup chicken broth
4) 1 teaspoon Italian seasoning

In saucepan cook carrots and zucchini in chicken broth until just tender. Drain and return vegetables to saucepan. Add seasoning and toss gently. 4 Servings.

Per Serving:

Calories	24.89	Protein	1.23g
Total Fat	0.27g	Carbohydrate	4.77g
Saturated Fat	0.07g	Cholesterol	0mg
Sodium	111.9mg	Fiber	1.43g

Carrot Casserole

1) 1 pound package mini-carrots, sliced
2) 1/2 cup low-fat Swiss cheese, shredded
3) 1/4 teaspoon ground nutmeg
4) 1 cup fat-free chicken broth

Cook carrots in broth until tender. Drain and retain broth. Mash carrots. Combine mashed carrots, cheese and nutmeg. Add some of the broth (1/2 cup) to make carrots creamy. Place in casserole and bake at 350 degrees for 15 to 20 minutes. 4 Servings.

Per Serving:

Calories	96.26	Protein	6.17g
Total Fat	2.72g	Carbohydrate	11.75g
Saturated Fat	0.03g	Cholesterol	8.50mg
Sodium	254.7mg	Fiber	3.40g

Braised Celery

1)   2 cups celery sticks
2)   1/2 cup beef bouillon
3)   2 tablespoons chopped fresh parsley
4)   1 tablespoon low-fat margarine

Combine above ingredients and place in 1-quart casserole. Bake at 400 degrees for 30 minutes. 4 Servings.

Per Serving:

Calories	25.08	Protein	0.67g
Total Fat	1.56g	Carbohydrate	2.51g
Saturated Fat	0.29g	Cholesterol	0mg
Sodium	255.7mg	Fiber	1.02g

Southwestern Corn

1)   2 (15.25 ounce) cans corn, drained
2)   1 red bell pepper, chopped
3)   1/4 cup chopped onions
4)   Non-fat butter spray

Spray nonstick skillet with butter spray. Saute pepper and onions in butter spray until soft. Add corn and cook over low heat for 10 minutes. 6 Servings.

Per Serving:

Calories	122.9	Protein	3.97g
Total Fat	1.48g	Carbohydrate	28.23g
Saturated Fat	0.23g	Cholesterol	0mg
Sodium	466.9mg	Fiber	3.26g

Spicy Corn Bake

1) 2 (15.25 ounce) cans corn, drained
2) 1/2 cup sliced onion
3) 1 tablespoon prepared mustard
4) 1/2 cup chili sauce

Combine above ingredients and place into a casserole. Bake at 350 degrees for 25 minutes. 6 Servings.

Per Serving:

Calories	144.9	Protein	4.57g
Total Fat	1.55g	Carbohydrate	33.07g
Saturated Fat	0.23g	Cholesterol	0mg
Sodium	760.4mg	Fiber	3.14g

Italian Eggplant

1) 1 small eggplant
2) 1/4 cup Egg Beaters
3) 1/2 cup Italian seasoned bread crumbs
4) 1 1/2 cups spaghetti sauce

Spray nonstick skillet with cooking spray. Remove peel of eggplant and slice into circles. Dip circle in Egg Beater then into bread crumbs. Place each round in skillet and brown on both sides. Place in ovenproof casserole, putting a generous tablespoon of spaghetti sauce on each eggplant round. Stack if necessary. Bake covered at 350 degrees for 30 minutes. 4 Servings.

Per Serving:

Calories	121.4	Protein	5.06g
Total Fat	2.65g	Carbohydrate	19.34g
Saturated Fat	0.10g	Cholesterol	0.22mg
Sodium	872.8mg	Fiber	1.20g

Garlic Green Beans

1)   1 (10 ounce) package frozen Italian style green beans
2)   2 teaspoons olive oil
3)   2 garlic cloves, crushed
4)   2 tablespoons grated Parmesan cheese

In nonstick skillet over medium heat, combine beans, olive oil and garlic. Bring to a boil. Cover, reduce heat and simmer 5 minutes. Remove cover, stir and cook 3 minutes longer or until liquid evaporates. Season to taste and sprinkle with Parmesan cheese. 4 Servings.

Per Serving:

Calories	61.97	Protein	2.10g
Total Fat	4.13g	Carbohydrate	4.93g
Saturated Fat	0.93g	Cholesterol	1.97mg
Sodium	56.04mg	Fiber	1.17g

Green Beans with Dill

1)   2 (14 1/2 ounce) cans French style green beans
2)   1/2 cup fresh mushrooms, sliced
3)   1 teaspoon fat-free margarine
4)   1 1/2 teaspoons dried dillweed

Warm beans over medium to low heat. Add mushrooms and cook 1 minute longer. Drain and toss with margarine and dill. 6 Servings.

Per Serving:

Calories	22.33	Protein	1.29g
Total Fat	0.16g	Carbohydrate	5.08g
Saturated Fat	0.03g	Cholesterol	0mg
Sodium	7.99mg	Fiber	1.17g

Tangy Italian Mushrooms

1)   2 cups fresh mushrooms, sliced
2)   1/2 cup fat-free Italian dressing
3)   1 large onion, chopped
4)   Butter spray

Marinate mushrooms in dressing for at least 1 hour or overnight, stirring occasionally. In nonstick skillet saute onion in butter spray. Drain mushrooms and add to onions. Continue to cook over medium heat until mushrooms are tender, but not limp. 6 Servings.

Per Serving:

Calories	24.01	Protein	0.80g
Total Fat	0.14g	Carbohydrate	4.73g
Saturated Fat	0.02g	Cholesterol	0mg
Sodium	282.3mg	Fiber	0.76g

Scalloped Potatoes

1)   3 medium potatoes, thinly sliced
2)   1/3 cup grated Parmesan cheese
3)   2/3 cup skim milk
4)   1/2 teaspoon paprika

Layer potatoes and cheese in a 2-quart casserole sprayed with cooking spray. Pour milk over potatoes and sprinkle with paprika. Cover and vent. Cook in microwave for 12 minutes. Take out, remove cover and broil 2 to 3 minutes to brown. 4 Servings.

Per Serving:

Calories	146.2	Protein	6.33g
Total Fat	2.17g	Carbohydrate	25.79g
Saturated Fat	1.34g	Cholesterol	5.93mg
Sodium	148.7mg	Fiber	2.11g

Herbed New Potatoes

1)   2 (15 ounce) cans new potatoes
2)   1 tablespoon minced parsley
3)   1 tablespoon minced chives
4)   1 tablespoon fat-free margarine

Heat potatoes in medium saucepan. Drain and add remaining ingredients, toss until potatoes are coated. 4 Servings.

Per Serving:

Calories	86.30	Protein	2.89g
Total Fat	0.32g	Carbohydrate	18.41g
Saturated Fat	0.08g	Cholesterol	0mg
Sodium	662.5mg	Fiber	3.40g

Potatoes O'Brien

1)   2 (15 ounce) cans sliced new potatoes, drained
2)   1/2 onion, finely minced
3)   1/2 green pepper, diced
4)   2 tablespoons fat-free margarine

Melt margarine in nonstick skillet. Add onions and green pepper and cook over medium heat until tender. Add drained potatoes and continue to saute for 5 minutes. Pepper to taste. Place in 9-inch sprayed pie plate and bake for 15 minutes at 350 degrees. 4 Servings.

Per Serving:

Calories	97.65	Protein	3.21g
Total Fat	0.37g	Carbohydrate	20.73g
Saturated Fat	0.09g	Cholesterol	0mg
Sodium	685.8mg	Fiber	3.93g

Roasted New Potatoes

1) 4 medium new potatoes, quartered
2) 2 tablespoons fat-free margarine
3) 3 small onions, quartered
4) 1/2 teaspoon marjoram

Melt margarine and add to a 2-quart casserole. Stir in marjoram.
Add potatoes and onions and toss in melted mixture until coated.
Cover dish and bake at 400 degrees for 1 to 1 1/2 hours.
4 Servings.

Per Serving:

Calories	81.76	Protein	1.81g
Total Fat	0.13g	Carbohydrate	18.29g
Saturated Fat	0.03g	Cholesterol	0mg
Sodium	49.02mg		
		Fiber	1.94g

Spicy New Potatoes

1) 8 small new potatoes
2) 1 teaspoon concentrated instant liquid crab and shrimp boil
3) 4 cups water
4) Pepper to taste

Pour crab boil, and pepper if desired, into water and bring to a
boil. Puncture potatoes and add to boiling water. Reduce heat
and simmer until potato skins barely pop and potatoes are tender,
around 20 minutes. 4 Servings.

Per Serving:

Calories	67.86	Protein	1.46g
Total Fat	0.08g	Carbohydrate	15.70g
Saturated Fat	0.02g	Cholesterol	0mg
Sodium	3.12mg	Fiber	1.40g

Mashed Potatoes and Carrots

1)   4 potatoes, peeled and cut into chunks
2)   1 large carrot, peeled and cut into chunks
3)   1/3 cup skim milk
4)   1 teaspoon dried dill leaves

In boiling water, add potatoes and carrot and cook for 25 minutes or until tender. Drain. Return to pot and mash. Stir in milk and dill. Season to taste. 6 Servings.

Per Serving:

Calories	66.59	Protein	1.72g
Total Fat	0.11g	Carbohydrate	15.05g
Saturated Fat	0.04g	Cholesterol	0.24mg
Sodium	18.81mg	Fiber	1.60g

Cottage Cheese Stuffed Baked Potatoes

1)   2 baking potatoes, baked
2)   1 cup low-fat cottage cheese
3)   1 tablespoon chives
4)   1 teaspoon onion powder

Bake potatoes in 425 degree oven for 1 hour. Cut potatoes in half lengthwise and scoop out insides. Return shell to oven and bake until crisp. Whip potato insides with remaining ingredients and put mixture into potato skins. Return to oven and bake until thoroughly heated. 4 Servings.

Per Serving:

Calories	151.0	Protein	9.32g
Total Fat	0.68g	Carbohydrate	27.02g
Saturated Fat	0.39g	Cholesterol	2.49mg
Sodium	237.5mg	Fiber	2.42g

Stuffed Baked Potatoes

1)   4 baking potatoes, baked
2)   1/2 cup skim milk
3)   2 tablespoons fat-free margarine
4)   1/4 cup low-fat cheddar cheese

Cut baked potatoes in half lengthwise. Scoop potato out of skin leaving shell intact. Mash potato pulp with milk and margarine. Stir in cheese. Refill potato shells with mixture and reheat briefly at 350 degrees until warm. 8 Servings.

Per Serving:

Calories	136.7	Protein	4.85g
Total Fat	1.38g	Carbohydrate	26.47g
Saturated Fat	0.04g	Cholesterol	5.28mg
Sodium	73.47mg	Fiber	2.42g

Gingered Sweet Potatoes

1)   2 medium sweet potatoes, peeled and diced
2)   1 tablespoon low-fat margarine
3)   1 teaspoon brown sugar
4)   1/4 teaspoon ground ginger or pumpkin pie spice

Arrange potatoes in a steaming rack. Place over boiling water; cover and steam until tender. Remove and place in serving dish. Combine remaining ingredients, blend well. Toss with the hot sweet potatoes. 4 Servings.

Per Serving:

Calories	193.2	Protein	2.71g
Total Fat	1.87g	Carbohydrate	42.02g
Saturated Fat	0.33g	Cholesterol	0mg
Sodium	54.70mg	Fiber	4.10g

Baked Sweet Potatoes

1) 2 (15 ounce) cans sweet potatoes with juice, cut into
        1/2 inch chunks
2) 1/2 cup firmly packed brown sugar
3) 1/4 cup fat-free margarine, melted
4) 1/2 teaspoon cinnamon

Layer potatoes, brown sugar and margarine in a casserole.
Sprinkle with cinnamon. Bake uncovered at 375 degrees for
30 minutes. 8 Servings.

Per Serving:

Calories	131.6	Protein	1.05g
Total Fat	0.22g	Carbohydrate	31.18g
Saturated Fat	0.05g	Cholesterol	0mg
Sodium	95.35mg	Fiber	1.99g

Cottaged Sweet Potatoes

1) 4 sweet potatoes, peeled and cut into strips
2) 2 tablespoons vegetable oil
3) 2 tablespoons Cajun spice seasoning
4) 1 tablespoon hot pepper sauce

Mix oil, Cajun spice and hot pepper sauce together. Add potatoes
and toss until well coated. Spread potatoes onto a nonstick pan
sprayed lightly with cooking spray. Bake at 400 degrees for
40 minutes, turning occasionally or until potatoes are tender.
8 Servings.

Per Serving:

Calories	133.1	Protein	1.72g
Total Fat	3.52g	Carbohydrate	24.27g
Saturated Fat	0.42g	Cholesterol	0mg
Sodium	1015mg	Fiber	3.00g

Garlic and Herb Cheese Rice

1) 1 (14 1/2 ounce) can fat-free chicken broth
2) 1 cup instant rice
3) 1 (5 ounce) package light garlic and herb soft spreadable cheese
4) 1/4 teaspoon ground pepper

Bring chicken broth to a boil and gradually stir in rice. Cook rice according to instructions on box. Remove from heat and stir in cheese and pepper until cheese is melted. 4 Servings.

Per Serving:

Calories	170.8	Protein	4.35g
Total Fat	5.07g	Carbohydrate	23.10g
Saturated Fat	3.15g	Cholesterol	12.50mg
Sodium	574.3mg	Fiber	0.42g

Sesame Rice

1) 4 cups cooked white rice
2) 1/4 cup green onions, chopped
3) 2 tablespoons sesame seeds
4) 1/4 cup low-sodium soy sauce

While rice is hot, combine all ingredients and place into serving dish. Stir well. 8 Servings.

Per Serving:

Calories	151.8	Protein	2.99g
Total Fat	1.30g	Carbohydrate	30.66g
Saturated Fat	0.21g	Cholesterol	0mg
Sodium	283.3mg	Fiber	0.08g

Veggie Rice

1)   3 cups cooked brown rice
2)   1 (9 ounce) can peas, drained
3)   2 tablespoons parsley
4)   2 tablespoons low-fat margarine

In medium saucepan, combine ingredients. Stir until the mixture is heated through. 6 Servings.

Per Serving:

Calories	115.5	Protein	4.46g
Total Fat	2.88g	Carbohydrate	29.96g
Saturated Fat	0.50g	Cholesterol	0mg
Sodium	142.2mg	Fiber	3.51g

Sherried Brown Rice Pilaf

1)   1 cup brown rice, uncooked
2)   2 cups fat-free chicken broth, plus 1 cup water
3)   3/4 cup fresh mushrooms, sliced
4)   3 tablespoons cooking sherry

In medium saucepan cook mushrooms in 2 tablespoons of water until slightly tender. Add rice. Stir in broth/water mixture and bring to a boil. Place into a 2-quart casserole, cover and bake at 350 degrees for 1 hour. Remove from heat and stir in sherry. Serve warm. 4 Servings.

Per Serving:

Calories	191.9	Protein	3.95g
Total Fat	1.40g	Carbohydrate	37.08g
Saturated Fat	0.28g	Cholesterol	0mg
Sodium	374.7mg	Fiber	1.77g

Skillet Squash

1) 1 medium acorn squash
2) 1/3 cup pineapple juice
3) 1 tablespoon light brown sugar
4) 1/4 teaspoon cinnamon

Cut squash crosswise into 1/2-inch slices and discard seeds.
Arrange in large skillet. In small bowl, combine juice, sugar and
cinnamon. Pour over squash rings. Bring to a boil and reduce
heat. Simmer, covered, for 25 minutes or until squash is tender.
Arrange squash on platter and pour remaining sauce over squash.
4 Servings.

Per Serving:

Calories	80.31	Protein	1.21g
Total Fat	0.16g	Carbohydrate	20.83g
Saturated Fat	0.03g	Cholesterol	0mg
Sodium	4.32mg	Fiber	0.10g

Candied Acorn Squash

1) 2 acorn squash
2) 4 tablespoons "lite" maple syrup
3) 2 teaspoons low-fat margarine
4) 1/4 teaspoon ground allspice

Cut squash in half and remove seeds and stringy parts. Place
halves, cut side up, in baking dish. Put 1 tablespoon syrup and
1/2 teaspoon margarine in each half. Sprinkle with allspice, cover
and bake at 375 degrees for 35 minutes. 8 Servings.

Per Serving:

Calories	74.79	Protein	1.17g
Total Fat	0.63g	Carbohydrate	18.15g
Saturated Fat	0.10g	Cholesterol	0mg
Sodium	37.91mg	Fiber	2.0g

Spinach Topped Tomatoes

1)   1 (10 ounce) package chopped spinach, cooked and
      drained
2)   1 teaspoon instant chicken bouillon
3)   1/4 teaspoon nutmeg
4)   3 medium tomatoes

Place spinach in medium bowl. Mix bouillon with 1/2 cup hot
water. Combine spinach with broth and nutmeg. Cut tomatoes
into halves crosswise and arrange, cut side up, on baking sheet.
Top each tomato half with 1/6 of the spinach mixture. Bake at
325 degrees for 30 minutes or until tomatoes are tender, but
retain their shape. 6 Servings.

Per Serving:

Calories	28.23	Protein	2.17g
Total Fat	0.35g	Carbohydrate	5.64g
Saturated Fat	0.06g	Cholesterol	0mg
Sodium	178.6mg	Fiber	2.10g

Herb Tomato Slices

1)   3 medium tomatoes
2)   2/3 cup fresh bread crumbs
3)   1 tablespoon fat-free margarine, melted
4)   1/4 teaspoon dried basil

Slice tomatoes and place in shallow baking dish. Mix bread
crumbs, margarine and basil. Sprinkle mixture over tomatoes and
bake, uncovered, at 350 degrees for 5 to 6 minutes or until
crumbs are brown. 6 Servings.

Per Serving:

Calories	52.68	Protein	1.76g
Total Fat	0.74g	Carbohydrate	10.00g
Saturated Fat	0.15	Cholesterol	0mg
Sodium	105.5mg	Fiber	1.09g

Marinated Vegetables

1) 1 (10 ounce) package frozen cut green beans
2) 1 (10 ounce) package frozen cauliflower
3) 1/4 cup fat-free Italian dressing
4) 1 (2 ounce) jar sliced pimiento, drained

Cook beans and cauliflower according to package directions.
Drain vegetables and place in mixing bowl. Add salad dressing
and pimiento. Toss until vegetables are coated. Cover and chill at
least 4 hours or overnight. 8 Servings.

Per Serving:

Calories	20.26	Protein	1.11g
Total Fat	0.10g	Carbohydrate	4.27g
Saturated Fat	0.01g	Cholesterol	0mg
Sodium	213.0mg	Fiber	1.35g

Zucchini Squash

1) 2 medium zucchini squash
2) I Can't Believe It's Not Butter Spray
3) 4 teaspoons Parmesan cheese
4) 4 teaspoons seasoned bread crumbs

dPlace zucchini on microwavable dish. Pierce with fork.
Microwave approximately 5 minutes on high or until tender but
not soft. Split in half lengthwise. Spray with butter spray.
Sprinkle each half with 1 teaspoon cheese and 1 teaspoon bread
crumbs. 4 Servings.

Per Serving:

Calories	23.43	Protein	1.71g
Total Fat	0.64g	Carbohydrate	3.24g
Saturated Fat	0.35g	Cholesterol	1.35mg
Sodium	81.56mg	Fiber	0.78g

Low-fat Recipe Samples From Volume I and II:

Squash Casserole

Volume I

1) 6 medium yellow squash
2) 1 small onion, chopped
3) 1 cup Healthy Choice fat-free cheese
4) 1 (4 ounce) can chopped green chiles

Boil squash and onion until tender. Drain well and mix with cheese and chiles. Pour into dish sprayed with cooking spray. Bake 15 minutes at 375 degrees. 8 Servings.

Per Serving:

Calories	44.55	Protein	5.44g
Total Fat	0.30g	Carbohydrate	5.74g
Saturated Fat	0.06g	Cholesterol	0mg
Sodium	56.20mg	Fiber	1.94g

Okra Succotash

Volume II

1) 3 cups sliced okra
2) 1 (16 ounce) can corn
3) 1 (14 1/2 ounce) can seasoned stewed tomatoes
4) 1/2 cup chopped onion

Rinse okra under running water. Drain. Combine ingredients in a large skillet. Cover and simmer for 15 minutes. Season to taste. 8 Servings.

Per Serving:

Calories	67.26	Protein	2.38g
Total Fat	0.31g	Carbohydrate	15.47g
Saturated Fat	0.05g	Cholesterol	0mg
Sodium	293.0mg	Fiber	1.55g

Main Dishes

Oven Fried Chicken

1)   6 (5 ounce) chicken breasts (boneless and skinless)
2)   1 cup crushed corn flakes
3)   1/4 cup buttermilk
4)   1 teaspoon Creole seasoning

Combine Creole seasoning and corn flake crumbs. Brush chicken with buttermilk and roll chicken in crumb mixture. Place chicken in baking dish and bake at 375 degrees for 1 hour. 6 Servings.

Per Serving:

Calories	228.1	Protein	32.93g
Total Fat	2.65g	Carbohydrate	16.80g
Saturated Fat	2.56g	Cholesterol	40.44mg
Sodium	758.9mg	Fiber	0.49g

Broiled and Spicy Chicken

1)   6 (5 ounce) chicken breasts (boneless and skinless)
2)   1/2 cup fat-free Italian dressing
3)   1 cup tomato juice
4)   1/2 teaspoon chili powder

Combine dressing, tomato juice and chili powder. Pour over chicken and marinate for several hours. Broil for 30 minutes or until done, turning once and basting frequently. 6 Servings.

Per Serving:

Calories	165.6	Protein	31.34g
Total Fat	2.56g	Carbohydrate	3.18g
Saturated Fat	2.50g	Cholesterol	40.00mg
Sodium	769.9mg	Fiber	0.24g

Tarragon Chicken

1) 6 (5 ounce) chicken breasts (boneless and skinless)
2) 1 cup white cooking wine
3) 1 tablespoon dried tarragon leaves
4) Black pepper, to taste

Combine wine, tarragon and pepper. Pour over chicken and marinate for several hours in refrigerator. Bake chicken at 350 degrees for 1 hour. 6 Servings.

Per Serving:

Calories	177.1	Protein	31.10g
Total Fat	2.51g	Carbohydrate	0.32g
Saturated Fat	2.51g	Cholesterol	40.08mg
Sodium	342.7mg	Fiber	0g

Orange Mint Chicken

1) 6 (5 ounce) chicken breasts (boneless and skinless)
2) 1 cup sugar-free orange marmalade
3) 2 tablespoons lemon juice
4) 2 teaspoons dried mint leaves

In small saucepan, combine orange marmalade, lemon juice and mint leaves. Cook over low heat until glaze is well heated. Place chicken on shallow baking pan sprayed with cooking spray. Broil unglazed chicken breasts for 8 minutes on each side. Brush glaze over both sides of chicken and continue broiling for 15 minutes longer, turning once. Brush glaze over chicken breasts several times during last few minutes. 6 Servings.

Per Serving:

Calories	215.3	Protein	31.02g
Total Fat	2.50g	Carbohydrate	15.80g
Saturated Fat	2.50g	Cholesterol	40.00mg
Sodium	340.1mg	Fiber	0.02g

Lemon Garlic Chicken

1) 4 (5 ounce) chicken breasts (boneless and skinless)
2) 1 clove garlic, minced
3) 1/2 cup fat-free chicken broth
4) 1 tablespoon lemon juice

Using nonstick skillet sprayed with cooking spray, slowly saute garlic over low heat. Add chicken and cook over medium heat about 10 minutes or until brown on both sides. Add broth and lemon juice. Heat to boiling and then reduce heat. Cover and simmer 10 to 15 minutes or until chicken is done. Remove chicken and keep warm. Cook or reduce remaining liquid in pan, around 3 minutes. Pour over chicken and serve. 4 Servings.

Per Serving:

Calories	153.3	Protein	31.06g
Total Fat	2.50g	Carbohydrate	0.70g
Saturated Fat	2.50g	Cholesterol	40.00mg
Sodium	432.7mg	Fiber	0.03g

Chicken Breasts with Mushrooms

1) 6 (5 ounce) chicken breasts (boneless and skinless)
2) 1 tablespoon basil
3) 1/4 pound fresh mushrooms, sliced
4) 3 tablespoons white cooking wine

On stove top place chicken breasts in nonstick skillet. Over low-medium heat brown chicken for 1 to 2 minutes. Add mushrooms, basil and wine and continue to cook for 30 minutes or until thoroughly cooked. Spoon sauce over breasts while cooking. 6 Servings.

Per Serving:

Calories	159.9	Protein	31.41g
Total Fat	2.58g	Carbohydrate	0.96g
Saturated Fat	2.51g	Cholesterol	40.00mg
Sodium	341.1mg	Fiber	0.23g

Cherry Chicken

1) 4 (5 ounce) chicken breasts (boneless and skinless)
2) 1 tablespoon lemon juice
3) 1/3 cup cherry preserves
4) Dash ground allspice

Pat chicken dry and place on rack of broiler pan. Broil 4 inches from heat for 6 minutes. Brush with lemon juice. Turn chicken over and brush with remaining juice and broil 6 to 9 minutes longer or until tender and no longer pink. In small saucepan heat cherry preserves and allspice. Spoon over chicken breasts and serve. 4 Servings.

Per Serving:

Calories	214.8	Protein	31.20g
Total Fat	2.55g	Carbohydrate	17.33g
Saturated Fat	2.50g	Cholesterol	40.00mg
Sodium	350.6mg	Fiber	0.31g

Savory Baked Lemon Chicken

1) 6 (5 ounce) chicken breasts (boneless and skinless)
2) 1 teaspoon garlic salt
3) Juice of 2 lemons
4) 1/4 cup melted fat-free margarine

Rub chicken with garlic salt and lemon juice. Place in baking dish and pour margarine over chicken. Bake at 350 degrees for 1 hour, basting often. 6 Servings.

Per Serving:

Calories	155.9	Protein	31.04g
Total Fat	2.50g	Carbohydrate	0.88g
Saturated Fat	2.50g	Cholesterol	40.00mg
Sodium	560.5mg	Fiber	0.04g

Lime Chicken

1) 4 (5 ounce) chicken breasts (boneless and skinless)
2) Juice of 3 limes
3) 2 tablespoons chopped garlic
4) 2 cups sliced mushrooms

Slice chicken into thin strips. Saute chicken and garlic in lime juice until chicken is tender. Add mushrooms and continue to cook until chicken is lightly browned. 4 Servings.

Per Serving:

Calories	175.5	Protein	32.28g
Total Fat	2.71g	Carbohydrate	6.05g
Saturated Fat	2.53g	Cholesterol	40.00mg
Sodium	342.8mg	Fiber	0.66g

Honey Chicken

1) 6 (5 ounce) chicken breasts (boneless and skinless)
2) 1/2 cup honey
3) 1/3 cup lemon juice
4) 1/4 cup soy sauce

Combine honey, lemon juice and soy sauce. Brush chicken with half of the mixture and bake at 350 degrees for 20 minutes. Brush with additional mixture and bake for an additional 35 minutes or until done. Baste frequently. 6 Servings.

Per Serving:

Calories	245.9	Protein	32.40g
Total Fat	2.51g	Carbohydrate	24.94g
Saturated Fat	2.50g	Cholesterol	40.00mg
Sodium	1013mg	Fiber	0.21g

Oven Barbecued Chicken

1) 4 (5 ounce) chicken breasts (boneless and skinless)
2) 1/2 cup jellied cranberry sauce
3) 1/4 cup tomato sauce
4) 2 tablespoons prepared mustard

Combine cranberry sauce, tomato sauce and mustard. Brush both sides of chicken breasts with mixture. Bake, uncovered, at 375 degrees for 30 minutes. Turn chicken, brush with barbecue mixture again and bake for an additional 20 minutes or until chicken is tender. 4 Servings.

Per Serving:

Calories	211.4	Protein	31.57g
Total Fat	2.85g	Carbohydrate	14.92g
Saturated Fat	2.52g	Cholesterol	40.00mg
Sodium	520.5mg	Fiber	0.58g

Orange Chicken

1) 4 (5 ounce) chicken breasts (boneless and skinless)
2) 1 cup sugar-free orange soda
3) 1/4 cup low sodium soy sauce
4) 4 to 6 green onions, finely chopped

Combine soda and soy sauce. Marinate chicken breasts in mixture at least 8 hours or overnight in refrigerator. Place chicken and marinade in large baking dish. Sprinkle with onions and bake at 350 degrees for 1 hour. Baste occasionally. 4 Servings.

Per Serving:

Calories	164.0	Protein	32.21g
Total Fat	2.54g	Carbohydrate	2.47g
Saturated Fat	2.51g	Cholesterol	40.00mg
Sodium	945.4mg	Fiber	0.46g

Crock Pot Chicken

1) 4 (5 ounce) chicken breasts (boneless and skinless)
2) 1 small cabbage, quartered
3) 1 pound package of mini-carrots
4) 2 (14 1/2 ounce) large cans Mexican flavored stewed
   tomatoes

Place above ingredients in crock pot. Cover and cook on low
6 to 7 hours. 4 Servings.

Per Serving:

Calories	266.0	Protein	34.34g
Total Fat	2.81g	Carbohydrate	26.77g
Saturated Fat	2.55g	Cholesterol	40.00mg
Sodium	970.8mg	Fiber	4.21g

Mexican Chicken

1) 4 (5 ounce) chicken breasts (boneless and skinless)
2) 1 (16 ounce) jar mild thick chunky salsa
3) 1 (2 1/4 ounce) can sliced black olives, drained
4) 1/2 teaspoon finely chopped garlic

Beat chicken breasts to uniform thickness. Spray nonstick frying
pan with olive oil flavored spray. Saute garlic over low heat. Add
chicken and over low-medium heat cook until golden, turning
once. Add salsa and cover. Continue to cook over low-medium
heat 30 to 40 minutes. Good served over rice. Top with olives.
4 Servings.

Per Serving:

Calories	270.6	Protein	47.23
Total Fat	4.21g	Carbohydrate	9.49g
Saturated Fat	2.73g	Cholesterol	60.00mg
Sodium	1279mg	Fiber	0.03g

Cranberry Chicken

1) 6 (5 ounce) chicken breasts (skinless and boneless)
2) 1 (8 ounce) bottle fat-free Catalina salad dressing
3) 1 package dry onion soup mix
4) 1 (16 ounce) can whole cranberry sauce

Combine Catalina dressing, onion soup and whole cranberry sauce. Pour over chicken breasts. Place in refrigerator and marinate overnight or at least 2 hours. Remove from marinade, reserving marinade to brush chicken while baking. Bake uncovered for 45 minutes at 350 degrees. 6 Servings.

Per Serving:

Calories	323.9	Protein	31.91g
Total Fat	3.00g	Carbohydrate	40.53g
Saturated Fat	2.59g	Cholesterol	40.33mg
Sodium	1248mg	Fiber	1.43g

Mandarin Chicken Breasts

1) 4 (5 ounce) chicken breasts (skinless and boneless)
2) 1 envelope dry onion soup mix
3) 1 (8 ounce) can pineapple chunks, undrained
4) 1 (11 ounce) can mandarin orange, undrained

On stove top over low heat, brown chicken breasts in nonstick skillet. Combine onion soup mix, pineapple chunks and mandarin oranges. Pour over chicken breasts. Simmer for 30 to 40 minutes or until chicken is done. 4 Servings.

Per Serving:

Calories	263.7	Protein	32.82g
Total Fat	3.08g	Carbohydrate	26.47g
Saturated Fat	2.63g	Cholesterol	40.49mg
Sodium	1232mg	Fiber	2.20g

Italian Chicken

1) 4 (5 ounce) chicken breasts (skinless and boneless)
2) 1 cup fat-free Italian dressing
3) 1 teaspoon lemon pepper
4) 1/8 teaspoon salt

Combine Italian dressing, lemon pepper and salt. Pour over chicken breasts and marinate for 2 hours or more in refrigerator. Remove chicken from marinade and bake uncovered at 350 degrees for 45 minutes. Broil for last 5 minutes. 4 Servings.

Per Serving:

Calories	174.00	Protein	31.00g
Total Fat	2.50g	Carbohydrate	4.00g
Saturated Fat	2.50g	Cholesterol	40.00mg
Sodium	1333mg	Fiber	0g

Chicken and Rice

1) 8 (5 ounce) chicken breasts (boneless and skinless)
2) 2 (6.2 ounce) boxes Uncle Ben's Wild Rice Mix
3) 1 (4 ounce) can sliced mushrooms
4) 1 (11 ounce) can mandarin oranges

Place rice in bottom of roaster with cover. Sprinkle with 1 of the seasoning packets in rice. Lay chicken over rice. Pour mushrooms and oranges with juice over chicken. Sprinkle top with second seasoning packet. Add water, according to package directions, to cover rice. Cover and bake at 350 degrees about 2 hours. Remove cover for last 20 minutes. 8 Servings.

Per Serving:

Calories	252.2	Protein	33.86g
Total Fat	2.73g	Carbohydrate	22.95g
Saturated Fat	2.51g	Cholesterol	40.00mg
Sodium	639.6mg	Fiber	1.06g

Honey Baked Chicken Breasts

1)   4 (5 ounce) chicken breasts (skinless and boneless)
2)   1/2 cup honey
3)   1/2 cup Dijon mustard
4)   1 cup seasoned bread crumbs

Combine honey and mustard. Dip chicken in honey mixture and roll in bread crumbs. Place on foil covered baking pan. Bake at 400 degrees for 30 minutes. Spoon remaining honey mixture over chicken breasts and continue to bake for 10 to 15 minutes.
4 Servings.

Per Serving:

Calories	345.0	Protein	34.21g
Total Fat	3.07g	Carbohydrate	38.33g
Saturated Fat	2.66g	Cholesterol	40.44mg
Sodium	1644mg	Fiber	0.06g

Tasty Chicken

1)   4 (5 ounce) chicken breasts (skinless and boneless)
2)   1/3 cup tomato juice
3)   1/2 teaspoon garlic powder
4)   1/2 teaspoon oregano

Pound chicken with meat tenderizer mallet until uniform thickness. Roll chicken breasts in tomato juice. Place chicken on foil in baking dish and sprinkle with garlic and oregano mixture. Bake uncovered at 350 degrees for 45 minutes. 4 Servings.

Per Serving:

Calories	155.2	Protein	31.23g
Total Fat	2.53g	Carbohydrate	1.23g
Saturated Fat	2.51g	Cholesterol	40.00mg
Sodium	412.8mg	Fiber	0.12g

Baked Chimichangas

1) 8 (6 inch) fat-free flour tortillas
2) 1 1/2 cups cooked and cubed chicken
3) 2 ounces grated low-fat cheese
4) 3/4 cup thick and chunky salsa

Mix chicken, cheese and salsa. Warm tortillas until pliable in 400 degree oven or 5 seconds each in microwave. Dampen one side of tortilla with water and place wet side down. Spoon on chicken mixture. Fold to hold in filling. Spray baking dish with nonstick cooking spray. Lay chimichangas, seam side down, on baking dish. Bake for 15 minutes. 4 Servings.

Per Serving:

Calories	317.5	Protein	30.68g
Total Fat	4.35g	Carbohydrate	35.43g
Saturated Fat	2.02g	Cholesterol	56.22mg
Sodium	844.2mg	Fiber	0g

Rolled Chicken and Asparagus

1) 4 (5 ounce) chicken breasts (boneless and skinless)
2) 30 asparagus spears, tough ends removed
3) 2 tablespoons lemon juice
4) 6 green onions, chopped

Cut chicken breasts into 8 or 10 strips, each about 1x5-inches long. Wrap each strip in a corkscrew fashion around 2 or 3 asparagus spears. Fasten with toothpicks. Place in a covered baking dish that has been sprayed with a nonstick cooking spray. Sprinkle with lemon juice and onions. Cover and bake at 350 degrees for 30 minutes. Remove toothpicks. Serve hot or refrigerate until chilled and serve cold. 4 Servings.

Per Serving:

Calories	180.8	Protein	33.73g
Total Fat	2.74g	Carbohydrate	6.47g
Saturated Fat	2.55g	Cholesterol	40.00mg
Sodium	344.2mg	Fiber	2.63

Yogurt Cumin Chicken

1) 4 (5 ounce) chicken breasts (boneless and skinless)
2) 1/3 cup non-fat yogurt
3) 1/4 cup apricot jam
4) 1 teaspoon cumin

Place chicken in baking dish that has been sprayed with cooking spray. Bake, uncovered, for 30 minutes at 350 degrees. Mix yogurt, apricot jam and cumin. Spoon over chicken. Bake for 15 minutes or until chicken is no longer pink and sauce is heated. 4 Servings.

Per Serving:

Calories	209.6	Protein	32.36g
Total Fat	2.54g	Carbohydrate	14.57g
Saturated Fat	2.50g	Cholesterol	40.47mg
Sodium	373.0mg	Fiber	0.24g

Sausage and Sauerkraut

1) 1 pound smoked turkey sausage
2) 1 (32 ounce) jar sauerkraut, drained
3) 2 cups unpeeled potatoes, thinly sliced
4) 1/2 cup thinly sliced onion

Place sauerkraut in large casserole. Top with onions and potatoes. Cut sausage into serving pieces (about 10) and place on top of potatoes and onions. Cover and cook at 350 degrees for 1 hour or until potatoes are tender. 8 Servings.

Per Serving:

Calories	142.0	Protein	11.24
Total Fat	5.07g	Carbohydrate	13.67g
Saturated Fat	1.27g	Cholesterol	36.45mg
Sodium	1236mg	Fiber	3.61g

Mary's White Chili

1) 1 pound ground turkey
2) 2 (15 ounce) cans great northern beans
3)· 1 (16 ounce) can white hominy
4) 1 package Lawry's chili seasoning

Brown turkey in nonstick skillet. Drain any fat from pan. Add undrained beans and hominy. Combine chili seasoning with the 1/2 cup water called for in package and add to turkey chili. Bring to a boil, reduce heat and simmer for 20 minutes and until thoroughly heated. 8 Servings.

Per Serving:

Calories	264.4	Protein	19.19g
Total Fat	5.82g	Carbohydrate	33.77g
Saturated Fat	1.47g	Cholesterol	44.79mg
Sodium	463.0mg	Fiber	6.63g

Low-fat Recipe Samples from Volume I and II:

Worcester Chicken

Volume I

1) 6 (5 ounce) chicken breasts (skinned and boned)
2) 1/4 cup Worcestershire sauce
3) 1/2 cup fat-free margarine
4) 2 tablespoons lemon pepper

Place chicken in large casserole sprayed with cooking spray. Spread margarine on each piece of chicken. Sprinkle with lemon pepper and Worcestershire sauce. Bake, uncovered, at 350 degrees for 1 hour. 6 Servings.

Per Serving:

Calories	160.0	Protein	31.00g
Total Fat	2.50g	Carbohydrate	0.67g
Saturated Fat	2.50g	Cholesterol	40.00mg
Sodium	824.3mg	Fiber	0g

Confetti Chicken

Volume II

1) 1 1/2 cups chicken, cooked and cubed
2) 2 (14 1/2 ounce) cans seasoned tomatoes/onions
3) 1 green pepper, chopped
4) 2 cups rice, cooked

In skillet, combine first three ingredients and season to taste. Simmer for 15 minutes. Serve over rice. 4 Servings.

Per Serving:

Calories	279.6	Protein	19.40g
Total Fat	2.32g	Carbohydrate	43.86g
Saturated Fat	0.65g	Cholesterol	40.43mg
Sodium	619.3mg	Fiber	0.33g

If you are trying to reduce the fat in your diet, always remove the skin of poultry before you cook it; choose oven frying over deep fat or skillet frying; choose chicken breasts over legs or thighs — the white meat contains less fat than dark meat.

Sweet Mustard Fish

1) 1 pound cod
2) 1/2 cup thick and chunky salsa
3) 2 tablespoons honey
4) 2 tablespoons Dijon mustard

Arrange fish in baking casserole that has been sprayed with
nonstick cooking spray. Bake at 450 degrees, uncovered, for
4 to 6 minutes. Drain any liquid. Combine remaining ingredients
and spoon over fish. Return to oven for 2 minutes to heat sauce.
4 Servings.

Per Serving:

Calories	157.4	Protein	24.23g
Total Fat	0.76g	Carbohydrate	10.65g
Saturated Fat	0.15g	Cholesterol	53.76mg
Sodium	441.7mg	Fiber	0.02g

Scallop Kabobs

1) 1 pound fresh sea scallops
2) 2 large green peppers, cut in 1 inch squares
3) 1 pint cherry tomatoes
4) 1 (8 ounce) bottle fat-free Italian salad dressing

Combine all ingredients in shallow dish. Cover and marinate
at least 3 hours, stirring occasionally. On skewers, alternate
scallops, green peppers, and cherry tomatoes. Place on broiler
rack and brush with remaining dressing. Broil 4 inches from heat
5 minutes, turn once and baste with dressing. 4 Servings.

Per Serving:

Calories	150.3	Protein	20.08g
Total Fat	1.21g	Carbohydrate	12.78g
Saturated Fat	0.14g	Cholesterol	37.42mg
Sodium	984.8mg	Fiber	1.60g

Baked Cod Vinaigrette

1) 1 pound cod fillets
2) 3 tablespoons fat-free vinaigrette dressing
3) Paprika
4) 1 tablespoon minced chives

Arrange fillets in shallow baking dish and brush with salad dressing. Sprinkle with paprika and chives. Bake, uncovered at 450 degrees for 10 to 12 minutes or until fillets flake with a fork. 4 Servings.

Per Serving:

Calories	98.84	Protein	20.22g
Total Fat	0.77g	Carbohydrate	1.16g
Saturated Fat	0.15g	Cholesterol	48.76mg
Sodium	211.3mg	Fiber	0.02g

Texas Boiled Beer Shrimp

1) 2 pounds unshelled large raw shrimp, deheaded
2) 2 (12 ounce) cans lite beer
3) 2 tablespoons crab boil seasoning
4) Pepper to taste (optional)

In large pot, bring beer to boil with seasonings. Stir in shrimp and cover. Return to boil and simmer for 5 minutes. Turn heat off and leave shrimp in hot beer for a few more minutes. Drain shrimp and serve immediately. Serve with lemon wedges and cocktail sauce. 4 Servings.

Per Serving:

Calories	240.4	Protein	46.06g
Total Fat	3.92g	Carbohydrate	2.06g
Saturated Fat	0.74g	Cholesterol	344.7g
Sodium	335.7mg	Fiber	0g

Spicy Shrimp

1) 1 pound large raw shrimp, peeled and cleaned
2) 1/2 cup fat-free margarine
3) 1/2 pound fresh mushrooms, sliced
4) Chili seasoning

Melt 1/4 cup of margarine in skillet and add shrimp. Saute shrimp just until tender and pink (about 5 minutes). Stir in remaining margarine and mushrooms and cook 5 minutes more. Sprinkle shrimp with chili seasoning (use like you would use pepper). Good served over rice. 4 Servings

Per Serving:

Calories	240.4	Protein	46.06g
Total Fat	3.92g	Carbohydrate	2.06g
Saturated Fat	0.74g	Cholesterol	344.7mg
Sodium	335.7mg	Fiber	0g

Broiled Shrimp

1) 1 pound shrimp, cleaned and peeled
2) 2 tablespoons olive oil
3) 2 tablespoons minced garlic
4) 4 teaspoons chopped parsley

Combine olive oil, garlic and parsley. Roll the shrimp in mixture and broil until pink (about 5 minutes). 4 Servings.

Per Serving:

Calories	190.8	Protein	23.52g
Total Fat	8.75g	Carbohydrate	3.43g
Saturated Fat	1.29g	Cholesterol	172.4mg
Sodium	169.6mg	Fiber	0.15g

Orange Roughy with Red Peppers

1) 1 pound orange roughy
2) 1 small onion, cut into thin slices
3) 2 medium red bell peppers, cut into strips
4) 1 teaspoon dried thyme leaves

Cut fillets into 4 serving pieces. Spray heated skillet with nonstick cooking spray. Layer onion and pepper in skillet. Sprinkle with 1/2 teaspoon thyme. Place fish over onion/pepper layer. Sprinkle with remaining thyme. Cover and cook over low heat 15 minutes. Uncover and cook until fish flakes easily with fork (about 10 minutes). 4 Servings.

Per Serving:

Calories	161.4	Protein	17.26g
Total Fat	8.07g	Carbohydrate	4.33g
Saturated Fat	0.17g	Cholesterol	22.68mg
Sodium	72.97mg	Fiber	1.17g

Company Halibut Steaks

1) 4 (4 ounce) halibut steaks
2) 1/2 cup apricot preserves
3) 2 tablespoons white vinegar
4) 1/2 teaspoon dried tarragon leaves

Spray broiler pan rack with nonstick cooking spray. Place fish steaks on rack and broil 4 inches from heat for 4 minutes. Turn fish and broil 4 minutes longer. Mix remaining ingredients and spoon onto fish. Broil 1 minute longer or until fish flakes easily with fork. 4 Servings.

Per Serving:

Calories	222.6	Protein	23.88g
Total Fat	2.68g	Carbohydrate	26.20g
Saturated Fat	0.37g	Cholesterol	36.29mg
Sodium	77.31mg	Fiber	0.48g

Tarragon Fish

1) **1 pound fish fillets**
2) **1/2 cup plain non-fat yogurt**
3) **1 teaspoon dried tarragon**
4) **1 ounce grated reduced fat mozzarella cheese**

Arrange fish in baking casserole that has been sprayed with nonstick cooking spray. Bake at 450 degrees, uncovered, for 4 to 5 minutes. Drain any liquid. Mix remaining ingredients and spread over fish. Bake 2 minutes or until cheese is melted. 4 Servings.

Per Serving:

Calories	129.2	Protein	24.26g
Total Fat	1.74g	Carbohydrate	2.70g
Saturated Fat	0.09g	Cholesterol	46.83mg
Sodium	135.8mg	Fiber	0.03g

Broiled Salmon Steaks

1) **2 (8 ounce) salmon steaks, halved**
2) **Non-fat butter spray**
3) **1 teaspoon dried marjoram**
4) **Freshly ground pepper**

Spray salmon with non-fat butter flavored spray. Sprinkle with 1/2 marjoram and pepper. Spray broiler rack with nonstick spray. Broil steaks 4 inches from heat source until first side is lightly browned (5 to 8 minutes). Spray, turn, and sprinkle with remaining half of marjoram and pepper. Broil 5 to 8 minutes longer or until fish flakes easily with fork. 4 Servings.

Per Serving:

Calories	204.5	Protein	22.77g
Total Fat	11.85g	Carbohydrate	0.09g
Saturated Fat	2.84g	Cholesterol	74.84mg
Sodium	53.41mg	Fiber	0.03g

Crunchy Baked Fish

1) 1 pound fish fillets
2) 1/3 cup finely crushed Cheez-It crackers
3) 1 teaspoon parsley flakes
4) 1/2 cup low-fat Catalina salad dressing

Preheat oven to 400 degrees. Mix crackers and parsley. Brush
both sides of fish with Catalina dressing. Coat one side of fish
with cracker mixture. Place fish, cracker side up, on cookie sheet
sprayed with nonstick cooking spray. Bake, uncovered, until fish
flakes easily with fork, 10 to 15 minutes. 4 Servings.

Per Serving:

Calories	137.8	Protein	20.33g
Total Fat	3.26g	Carbohydrate	6.89g
Saturated Fat	0.15g	Cholesterol	48.76mg
Sodium	318.2mg	Fiber	0g

Easy Cheesy Fish Fillets

1) 1 pound fish fillets
2) 1 onion, thinly sliced
3) 1/4 cup fat-free mayonnaise
4) 1/4 cup grated fat-free flavored cheese product

Place fillets in a single layer in baking casserole. Spread with
mayonnaise and sprinkle with cheese. Top with onions. Cover
and bake at 450 degrees for 10 minutes. Uncover and bake
4 to 6 minutes more, until browned. 4 Servings.

Per Serving:

Calories	122.7	Protein	22.68g
Total Fat	0.79g	Carbohydrate	4.98g
Saturated Fat	0.15g	Cholesterol	48.76mg
Sodium	251.8mg	Fiber	0.36g

Tangy Apricot Fish

1) 1 pound fish fillets
2) 1/3 cup non-fat yogurt
3) 3 tablespoons apricot jam
4) 1 tablespoon lemon juice

Arrange fish in baking casserole that has been sprayed with nonstick cooking spray. Bake at 450 degrees, uncovered, for 4 to 5 minutes. Drain any liquid. Mix remaining ingredients and pour over fish. Bake for 2 minutes longer to heat sauce. 4 Servings.

Per Serving:

Calories	137.7	Protein	21.24g
Total Fat	0.74g	Carbohydrate	11.06g
Saturated Fat	0.09g	Cholesterol	42.37mg
Sodium	97.69mg	Fiber	0.20g

Lemon Butter Dill Fish

1) 1 pound fish fillets
2) 3/4 cup fat-free lemon butter dill sauce for seafood
3) 1/4 cup thinly sliced red pepper
4) 1 tablespoon Parmesan cheese

Brush both sides of fish with 1/2 cup dill sauce. Arrange fish in baking casserole that has been sprayed with nonstick cooking spray. Place red pepper slices on top of fish. Drizzle rest of dill sauce over tops of fish and peppers. Sprinkle with Parmesan. Bake, uncovered, at 350 degrees for 20 minutes or until fish flakes easily with a fork. 4 Servings.

Per Serving:

Calories	140.4	Protein	21.57g
Total Fat	3.95g	Carbohydrate	4.45g
Saturated Fat	0.39g	Cholesterol	49.74mg
Sodium	593.6mg	Fiber	0.13g

Low-fat Recipe Samples from Volume I and II:

Barbequed Trout

Volume I

1) 4 trout
2) 4 tablespoons minced onion
3) 1 cup fat-free barbecue sauce
4) Salt and pepper

Place onion, barbecue sauce in body cavity of trout. Salt and pepper to taste. Wrap trout individually in foil and bake at 350 degrees for 20 minutes. 4 Servings.

Per Serving:

Calories	223.0	Protein	19.10g
Total Fat	4.11g	Carbohydrate	23.14g
Saturated Fat	1.15g	Cholesterol	94.12mg
Sodium	341.2mg	Fiber	0.18g

Baked Orange Roughy

Volume II

1) 1 pound orange roughy fillets
2) 1/4 cup lemon juice
3) 1/2 teaspoon tarragon leaves
4) 2 teaspoons dried mustard

Place fillets in large casserole that has been sprayed with nonstick cooking spray. Squeeze lemon juice over fillets. Sprinkle dried mustard and tarragon leaves over fish. Bake at 400 degrees for 25 minutes. 4 Servings.

Per Serving:

Calories	146.7	Protein	16.73g
Total Fat	7.94g	Carbohydrate	1.31g
Saturated Fat	0.15g	Cholesterol	22.68mg
Sodium	71.59mg	Fiber	0.06g

Spanish Fish

Volume II

1) 1 (1 pound) fish (snapper or redfish)
2) 1 bell pepper, chopped
3) 1 red onion, chopped
4) 1 (14 1/2 ounce) can seasoned tomatoes

Line shallow pan with foil leaving ample amount hanging over the edges. Pour 1/3 of the tomatoes onto the foil. Place fish over tomatoes. Sprinkle the bell pepper and onion over the fish. Pour remaining tomatoes over fish and loosely close up foil. Bake at 350 degrees for 20 minutes per pound or until fish is flaky.
4 Servings.

Per Serving:

Calories	167.8	Protein	24.89g
Total Fat	1.65g	Carbohydrate	12.52g
Saturated Fat	0.34g	Cholesterol	41.96mg
Sodium	366.9mg	Fiber	1.39

Most fish are excellent sources of low-fat protein and have fewer calories than other meats. The most important rule to remember when cooking seafood is to not overcook it. Also when buying fresh fish, refrigerate it in the coldest section of your refrigerator. If you don't plan to use it within a day or two, freeze it.

Sage Seasoned Pork Chops

1)   4 (1/2 inch) pork loin chops, trim fat
2)   1/2 teaspoon dried sage
3)   1 small onion, sliced and separated into rings
4)   2 apples, cored and cut into thin wedges

Rub sage onto both sides of chops. Place chops in a large skillet sprayed with nonstick cooking spray. Cook chops for 5 minutes on one side. Turn chops and add onion and apples. Cook for 7 minutes more or until chops are thoroughly cooked. 4 Servings.

Per Serving:

Calories	287.0	Protein	37.87g
Total Fat	8.88g	Carbohydrate	12.35g
Saturated Fat	3.02g	Cholesterol	107.2mg
Sodium	112.9mg	Fiber	2.25g

Best Pork Tenderloin

1)   1 1/2 pounds pork tenderloin
2)   1 teaspoon black pepper
3)   1 teaspoon rosemary leaves
4)   1 cup barbecue sauce

Rub tenderloin with pepper and rosemary leaves. Bake at 350 degrees for 1 1/2 hours. Slice and serve with warmed barbecue sauce. 6 Servings.

Per Serving:

Calories	185.8	Protein	24.09g
Total Fat	6.90g	Carbohydrate	5.34g
Saturated Fat	2.24g	Cholesterol	74.99mg
Sodium	395.9mg	Fiber	0.50g

Honey Mustard Pork Tenderloin

1) 2 (1 1/2 pound) pork tenderloins
2) 1/2 cup honey
3) 2 teaspoons prepared mustard
4) 1/4 cup brown sugar

Mix honey, mustard and brown sugar. Spread over pork tenderloins and let marinate at least 2 hours in refrigerator. Roast at 350 degrees for 1 hour. 12 Servings.

Per Serving:

Calories	182.2	Protein	19.41g
Total Fat	5.12g	Carbohydrate	14.46g
Saturated Fat	1.76g	Cholesterol	62.12mg
Sodium	56.51mg	Fiber	0.03g

Lemon and Garlic Roast Pork

1) 1 (3 pound) lean boneless pork loin roast
2) 3/4 teaspoon grated lemon rind
3) 3 garlic cloves, minced
4) 1 can low-salt chicken broth

Trim fat from pork. Combine lemon rind and garlic and rub evenly over pork. Place pork in a casserole dish and add broth. Bake at 400 degrees for 30 minutes. Turn pork over and bake an additional 35 minutes. Discard broth and serve. 12 Servings

Per Serving:

Calories	166.1	Protein	24.60g
Total Fat	6.51g	Carbohydrate	0.48g
Saturated Fat	2.20g	Cholesterol	66.64mg
Sodium	68.60mg	Fiber	0.02g

Deviled Pork Roast

1) 1 (3 pound) lean pork loin roast
2) 2 tablespoons Dijon mustard
3) 1 teaspoon ground thyme
4) Fresh ground pepper, to taste

Spread pork roast with thin coating of mustard. Sprinkle with thyme and pepper Roast, uncovered at 375 degrees for 1 1/2 hours. 12 Servings.

Per Serving:

Calories	164.3	Protein	24.21g
Total Fat	6.40g	Carbohydrate	0.07g
Saturated Fat	2.21g	Cholesterol	66.64mg
Sodium	118.6mg	Fiber	0.02g

Healthy Style Quesadillas

1) 4 fat-free flour tortillas
2) 4 teaspoons prepared honey mustard
3) 1 cup fat-free cheese, shredded
4) 4 slices 98% fat-free ham

Spread each tortilla with 1 teaspoon mustard. Sprinkle with cheese and top with 1 ham slice. Fold tortilla in half. In large nonstick skillet over medium-high heat. place one or two filled tortillas. Cook until cheese melts, about 1 minute per side. Serve with salsa if desired. 4 Servings.

Per Serving:

Calories	199.0	Protein	26.49g
Total Fat	1.42g	Carbohydrate	18.42g
Saturated Fat	0.46g	Cholesterol	13.32mg
Sodium	627.4mg	Fiber	0g

Baked Pork Tenderloin

1) 1 (1 1/2 pound) lean pork tenderloin
2) Butter flavored non-fat spray
3) 2 cups canned fat-free chicken broth
4) 1 (4 ounce) can mushroom stems and pieces

Brown meat in generous coating of butter flavored non-fat spray. Remove from skillet and place in casserole. Add a little flour to drippings and add chicken broth and mushrooms. Stir until heated and mixed. Pour over pork and bake at 350 degrees for 1 hour. 6 Servings.

Per Serving:

Calories	144.2	Protein	24.20g
Total Fat	3.93g	Carbohydrate	1.27g
Saturated Fat	1.35g	Cholesterol	73.86mg
Sodium	384.5mg	Fiber	0.45g

Pork Tenderloin Supreme

1) 2 (1 1/2 pound) lean pork tenderloin
2) 1 can tomato soup
3) 1 package onion soup mix
4) 2 tablespoons Worcestershire sauce

Place tenderloins in center of large sheet of tin foil. Mix remaining ingredients and spread over meat. Seal securely in foil. Place in shallow pan and bake for 2 hours at 325 degrees. Cut meat into 1-inch slices. Pour soup-gravy over slices of meat. 12 Servings.

Per Serving:

Calories	139.7	Protein	20.49g
Total Fat	3.78g	Carbohydrate	5.13g
Saturated Fat	1.22g	Cholesterol	61.30mg
Sodium	463.2mg	Fiber	0.36g

Marinated Pork Tenderloin

1)   1 (1 1/2 pound) pork tenderloin roast
2)   1 tablespoon sherry
3)   2 tablespoons low sodium soy sauce
4)   2 tablespoons brown sugar

Combine sherry, soy sauce and brown sugar. Rub over roast and marinate overnight in refrigerator. Roast at 300 degrees until tender 1 1/2 hours. 6 Servings.

Per Serving:

Calories	172.1	Protein	23.65g
Total Fat	6.15g	Carbohydrate	3.55g
Saturated Fat	2.13g	Cholesterol	74.99mg
Sodium	400.7mg	Fiber	0g

Pineapple Pork

1)   2 pounds lean pork shoulder meat, cut in 1 inch cubes
2)   1 (14 ounce) can pineapple chunks, drain and reserve liquid
3)   1/4 cup vinegar
4)   1 teaspoon ginger

Combine above ingredients and simmer in nonstick skillet for 1 hour. Add pineapple liquid if needed. Chill, skim off fat and reheat. Good served over rice. 8 Servings.

Per Serving:

Calories	195.9	Protein	22.19g
Total Fat	8.11g	Carbohydrate	7.16g
Saturated Fat	2.81g	Cholesterol	75.98mg
Sodium	90.71mg	Fiber	0.47g

Ham in Wine Sauce

1)   1 1/2 pounds lean cooked sliced ham
2)   1 cup currant jelly
3)   1 cup red cooking wine
4)   4 tablespoons sugar

Combine jelly, wine and sugar in saucepan. Cook over medium heat until mixture comes to a boil, stirring constantly. Continue to boil to a thick syrup. Serve over heated slices of ham. 8 Servings.

Per Serving:

Calories	252.7	Protein	16.80g
Total Fat	4.30g	Carbohydrate	33.08g
Saturated Fat	1.38g	Cholesterol	39.97mg
Sodium	1233mg	Fiber	0.44g

Raisin Spiced Ham Steak

1)   1 pound lean ready-to-eat ham steak
2)   1/2 teaspoon pumpkin pie spice
3)   1/2 cup unsweetened pineapple juice
4)   2 tablespoons (1 ounce) raisins

Brown and heat ham steak in a nonstick skillet sprayed with cooking spray. Remove steak to heated platter. Combine remaining ingredients and cook over high heat, stirring constantly, until mixture is reduced to a few tablespoons. Pour over ham steak. 4 Servings.

Per Serving:

Calories	212.2	Protein	22.46g
Total Fat	5.77g	Carbohydrate	17.19g
Saturated Fat	1.85g	Cholesterol	53.30mg
Sodium	1622mg	Fiber	0.49g

Hawaiian Pork Chops

1) 4 (1/2 inch thick) lean pork loin chops
2) 1 (8 ounce) can pineapple slices in own juice
3) 2 tablespoons brown sugar
4) 1/2 teaspoon ground nutmeg

Drain and reserve juice from canned pineapple. Place pork chops in baking dish that is lightly sprayed with cooking spray. Mix 3 tablespoons of the reserved pineapple juice with brown sugar and nutmeg. Spoon half of the mixture over the pork chops. Top with pineapple slices and spoon remaining mixture over pineapple. Cover and bake 30 minutes at 350 degrees. Uncover and bake 20 minutes longer, spoon sauce over chops occasionally. 4 Servings.

Per Serving:

Calories	305.9	Protein	37.86g
Total Fat	10.37g	Carbohydrate	13.45g
Saturated Fat	3.60g	Cholesterol	93.55mg
Sodium	78.92mg	Fiber	0.45g

Savory Broiled Pork Chops

1) 4 (5 ounce) lean pork loin chops (3/4-inch thick)
2) 3 tablespoons Dijon mustard
3) 1 teaspoon dried thyme
4) Freshly ground pepper

Spread half the mustard evenly over chops and sprinkle with half the thyme. Sprinkle with pepper. Broil 6 inches from heat 10 to 12 minutes. Turn chops and spread with remaining mustard and remaining thyme. Sprinkle with pepper. Broil second side until browned, around 10 to 12 minutes. 4 Servings.

Per Serving:

Calories	223.4	Protein	31.37g
Total Fat	8.55g	Carbohydrate	0.22g
Saturated Fat	2.94g	Cholesterol	77.96mg
Sodium	334.0mg	Fiber	0.07g

Orange Pork Chops

1) 4 lean pork rib chops
2) 1/3 cup light orange marmalade
3) 2 tablespoons Dijon mustard
4) 4 bunches green onions, chopped

In small saucepan mix marmalade and mustard and stir over medium heat until marmalade is melted. Set aside. Place chops on broiler rack. Broil chops about 4 inches from heat for 6 minutes; turn and broil for 2 more minutes. Spoon half of the glaze over chops and broil 5 minutes more or until chops are no longer pink. In separate skillet sprayed with nonstick cooking spray, stir-fry the onions 2 minutes or until crisp-tender. Stir in remaining glaze and heat thoroughly. Serve over pork chops. 4 Servings.

Per Serving:

Calories	278.3	Protein	38.49g
Total Fat	10.31g	Carbohydrate	4.00g
Saturated Fat	3.54g	Cholesterol	93.55mg
Sodium	264.2mg	Fiber	1.25g

Chinese Barbecued Pork

1) 1 1/2 pounds boneless pork tenderloin
2) 1/2 cup Chinese barbecue sauce
3) Bottled hot mustard

Marinate pork in barbecue sauce overnight in refrigerator. Remove from marinade and place pork in roasting pan. Roast pork for 1 1/2 hours at 325 degrees or until meat juices run clear. Slice 1/8-inch thick and refrigerate until ready to serve. Serve pork with hot mustard. 6 Servings.

Per Serving:

Calories	260.1	Protein	24.67g
Total Fat	8.70g	Carbohydrate	18.54g
Saturated Fat	2.54g	Cholesterol	70.19mg
Sodium	811.4mg	Fiber	0g

Ham and Potatoes O'Brien Casserole

1) 4 slices fat-free ham luncheon meat, cubed
2) 1 (24 ounce) package Oreida Frozen Potatoes O'Brien, thawed
3) 1 (8 ounce) package fat-free cream cheese, room temperature
4) 1 (4.5 ounce) can chopped green chilies

Preheat oven to 400 degrees. Combine cream cheese and green chilies. Pour over potatoes and ham and stir until well mixed. Place in 1-quart ovenproof casserole that has been sprayed with cooking spray. Bake 40 minutes. Pepper to taste. 4 Servings.

Per Serving:

Calories	142.8	Protein	0.00g
Total Fat	0.94g	Carbohydrate	23.83g
Saturated Fat	0.31g	Cholesterol	8.90mg
Sodium	563.6mg	Fiber	3.26g

Minted Lamb Patties

1) 1 pound lean ground lamb
2) 1/4 cup dry bread crumbs
3) 2 tablespoons dried mint
4) 1 teaspoon lemon pepper

Mix all ingredients thoroughly and shape into 4 patties. Spray broiler pan with nonstick cooking spray. Broil patties about 3 inches from heat for about 8 to 10 minutes or until no longer pink inside, turning once. 4 Servings.

Per Serving:

Calories	183.9	Protein	24.37g
Total Fat	7.03g	Carbohydrate	3.99g
Saturated Fat	2.48g	Cholesterol	74.84mg
Sodium	204.5mg	Fiber	0.23g

Lamb with Yogurt-Mint Sauce

1) 4 lamb loin chops, fat trimmed
2) 1/3 cup plain non-fat yogurt
3) 1/4 cup mint jelly
4) 2 tablespoons jalapeno jelly

Blend yogurt, mint and jalapeno jellies and save for sauce.
Spray broiler pan with nonstick cooking spray. Broil lamb chops
3 inches from heat for 12 to 14 minutes, turning chops after
6 minutes. Serve with sauce. 4 Servings.

Per Serving:

Calories	352.0	Protein	34.96g
Total Fat	15.73g	Carbohydrate	16.81g
Saturated Fat	5.63g	Cholesterol	112.6mg
Sodium	140.4mg	Fiber	0g

Low-fat Recipe Samples from Volume I and II:

Roast Pork in Marinade

Volume I

1) 4 pounds lean pork roast
2) 1 (15 ounce) can tomatoes, chopped
3) 1/4 cup white vinegar
4) 1/4 cup water

Place roast in roasting pan. Mix and pour the remaining
ingredients over roast. Best marinated overnight. Cover and bake
at 350 degrees for 4 hours. 10 Servings.

Per Serving:

Calories	268.8	Protein	39.28g
Total Fat	10.37g	Carbohydrate	2.18g
Saturated Fat	3.55g	Cholesterol	107.0mg
Sodium	163.7mg	Fiber	0.43g

Grilled Pork Chops

Volume II

1) 4 (1 inch thick) pork chops
2) 1/4 teaspoon salt
3) 3/4 teaspoon lemon pepper
4) 1/2 teaspoon dried whole oregano leaves

Mix salt, lemon pepper and oregano. Coat pork chops. Grill over low to medium hot heat for 25 minutes or until chops are no longer pink. Turn once. 4 Servings.

Per Serving:

Calories	253.4	Protein	37.61g
Total Fat	10.22g	Carbohydrate	0g
Saturated Fat	3.52g	Cholesterol	93.55mg
Sodium	281.9mg	Fiber	0g

―――

The Other White Meat:
Pork is a white meat, not only in terms of color, but more importantly because it is a lean meat that is low in fat and calories. America's pork producers have reduced the average fat content of pork by 31 percent and lowered average calories by 14 percent according to USDA figures. There are eight pork cuts that are lower than skinless chicken thigh in terms of fat and cholesterol content. The tenderloin is the leanest cut of pork.

Broiled Flank Steak

1) 1 1/2 pounds lean beef flank steak
2) 3/4 cup dry red wine or cooking wine
3) 1 1/2 teaspoons lemon pepper
4) 1 teaspoon garlic

Combine wine, garlic and lemon pepper; pour over steak.
Cover and marinate in refrigerator overnight. Coat broiler rack
with cooking spray and place flank steak on rack. Let flank steak
return to room temperature. Broil 3 to 4 inches from heat for
5 to 7 minutes on each side. Slice steak across grain into thin
slices to serve. 8 Servings.

Per 3 ounce Serving:

Calories	155.6	Protein	17.64g
Total Fat	6.42g	Carbohydrate	0.84g
Saturated Fat	2.77g	Cholesterol	43.09mg
Sodium	144.7mg	Fiber	0g

Flank Steak and Spinach Pinwheels

1) 1 1/2 pounds lean beef flank steak
2) 1 (10 ounce) package frozen spinach, thawed and drained
3) 1/4 cup grated Parmesan cheese
4) 1/4 cup fat-free sour cream

Cut shallow diagonal cuts on one side of steak and pound to
3/8-inch thickness. Combine spinach, sour cream and cheese and
spread on cut side of steak. Starting at narrow end, roll up steak
and secure with toothpicks at 1-inch intervals. Cut into 1-inch
slices, (leaving picks in steak) and place pinwheels on broiler rack
sprayed with cooking spray. Broil 6 inches from heat 7 minutes
on each side. Remove picks and serve. 8 Servings.

Per 3 ounce Serving:

Calories	156.1	Protein	20.18
Total Fat	7.15g	Carbohydrate	2.24g
Saturated Fat	3.22g	Cholesterol	44.49mg
Sodium	142.9mg	Fiber	1.06g

Southwestern Beef Combo

1) 1/2 pound lean ground beef
2) 1 small onion, chopped
3) 3 cups frozen potatoes O'Brien, thawed
4) 1 cup salsa

Brown ground beef and onion in large skillet. Pour off any drippings. Stir in potatoes and cook over medium-high heat for 5 minutes, stirring occasionally. Stir in salsa and continue to cook 10 minutes longer. 6 Servings.

Per Serving:
Calories	178.5	Protein	12.87g
Total Fat	7.85g	Carbohydrate	13.84g
Saturated Fat	3.15g	Cholesterol	35.09mg
Sodium	307.1mg	Fiber	1.58g

Savory Chuck Steaks

1) 4 (6 ounce) boneless lean beef chuck eye steaks
2) 1/4 cup steak sauce
3) 2 tablespoons brown sugar
4) 3 tablespoons fresh lime juice

Combine steak sauce, brown sugar and lime juice, reserving 2 tablespoons of this marinade. Place beef in plastic bag and add remaining marinade, turning to coat. Close bag securely and marinate for 10 minutes. Pour off marinade and grill steaks for 14 to 20 minutes for rare to medium done. Brush with reserved 2 tablespoons of marinade during last 2 minutes of cooking. 4 Servings.

Per Serving:
Calories	342.8	Protein	49.36g
Total Fat	9.71g	Carbohydrate	11.45g
Saturated Fat	3.52g	Cholesterol	117.4mg
Sodium	257.3mg	Fiber	0.05g

Creole Pepper Steak

1)   1 pound beef top round steak (cut 1-inch thick)
2)   2 cloves garlic, crushed
3)   1 teaspoon dried thyme
4)   1 teaspoon red pepper

Combine garlic, thyme and red pepper. Press evenly into both sides of steak. Grill 12 to 14 minutes for rare to medium, turning once. Cut steak diagonally into thin slices to serve. 4 Servings.

Per Serving:

Calories	197.3	Protein	24.77g
Total Fat	9.94g	Carbohydrate	0.50g
Saturated Fat	4.13g	Cholesterol	68.04mg
Sodium	56.96mg	Fiber	0.03g

Orange Pepper Steaks

1)   4 (4 ounce) beef tenderloin steaks (cut 1-inch thick)
2)   1/2 cup sugar free orange marmalade
3)   4 teaspoons cider vinegar
4)   1/2 teaspoon ground ginger

Combine marmalade, vinegar and ginger. Place steaks on rack in broiler pan and brush top of steaks with half of marmalade mixture. Broil 3 inches from heat for 10 to 15 minutes, turning once. Brush with remaining marmalade mixture after turning. 4 Servings.

Per Serving:

Calories	265.0	Protein	24.41g
Total Fat	12.17g	Carbohydrate	12.30g
Saturated Fat	4.86g	Cholesterol	66.90mg
Sodium	66.95mg	Fiber	0g

Chuck Roast Steaks

1)   3 pounds boneless chuck roast, trim fat
2)   1 teaspoon pepper
3)   1 teaspoon garlic powder
4)   1 teaspoon onion powder

Combine pepper, garlic powder and onion powder. Sprinkle roast
with mixture. Place on rack in broiler pan. Broil 5 inches from
the heat 5 minutes per side. Remove from broiler, cool until it
can be cut easily. Slice roast crosswise about 1-inch thick. Place
slices under broiler until lightly brown, turn and brown other
side. 12 Servings.

Per Serving:

Calories	266.1	Protein	37.37g
Total Fat	11.67g	Carbohydrate	0.42g
Saturated Fat	4.43g	Cholesterol	114.1mg
Sodium	74.77mg	Fiber	0.06g

Flank Steak

1)   1 1/2 pounds lean beef flank steak
2)   1/4 cup fat-free margarine, melted
3)   1 teaspoon garlic powder
4)   1/2 cup dry sherry

Combine sherry, margarine and garlic. Pour half mixture over
beef and broil 3 inches from heat for 5 to 7 minutes. Turn, pour
remaining mixture over beef and broil for 3 more minutes. Slice
diagonally and serve. 8 Servings.

Per 3 ounce Serving:

Calories	152.5	Protein	17.36g
Total Fat	6.33g	Carbohydrate	0.84g
Saturated Fat	2.73g	Cholesterol	42.52mg
Sodium	108.5mg	Fiber	0g

Flank Steak Joy

1) 1 1/2 pounds lean flank steak
2) 2 tablespoons soy sauce
3) 1 tablespoon sherry
4) 1 teaspoon honey

Combine soy sauce, sherry and honey. Pour over steak. Marinate several hours in refrigerator. Line a shallow pan with foil and place steak on foil. Broil about 10 minutes on each side. 8 Servings.

Per 3 ounce Serving:

Calories	138.3	Protein	17.51g
Total Fat	6.33g	Carbohydrate	1.18g
Saturated Fat	2.73g	Cholesterol	42.52mg
Sodium	319.5mg	Fiber	0g

Beef Goulash

1) 2 pounds lean stew beef
2) 1 large onion, chopped
3) 1 (11.5 ounce) can V-8 vegetable juice
4) 1/2 teaspoon pepper

Brown meat and onions in nonstick skillet. Add V-8 vegetable juice and pepper. Cover and simmer 1 1/2 hours. Good served with noodles. 8 Servings.

Per Serving:

Calories	277.9	Protein	37.92g
Total Fat	11.35g	Carbohydrate	3.64g
Saturated Fat	4.30g	Cholesterol	114.5mg
Sodium	209.6mg	Fiber	0.36g

Company Beef Tenderloin

1) 6 (4 ounce) beef tenderloin steaks
2) 8 ounces fresh mushrooms, sliced
3) 1 large clove garlic, minced
4) 1 cup cooking sherry

In large nonstick skillet sprayed with cooking spray, saute mushrooms and garlic for 4 minutes. Add sherry and cook until liquid is reduced. Stir frequently, set aside and keep warm. Broil tenderloin steaks for 5 minutes on each side. Arrange on platter and pour heated sherried mushroom sauce over steaks. 6 Servings.

Per Serving:

Calories	289.3	Protein	32.93g
Total Fat	10.68g	Carbohydrate	3.48g
Saturated Fat	4.14g	Cholesterol	95.25mg
Sodium	76.45mg	Fiber	0.47g

Veal Marsala

1) 1 pound veal, thinly sliced
2) 1/4 cup flour
3) 2 tablespoons fat-free margarine
4) 1/2 cup Marsala wine

Lightly dredge sliced veal in flour. Brown veal in margarine in a heavy skillet. Add Marsala wine. Cover pan and simmer over low heat for 5 minutes. 4 Servings.

Per Serving:

Calories	176.1	Protein	23.77g
Total Fat	3.01g	Carbohydrate	6.33g
Saturated Fat	0.90g	Cholesterol	89.58mg
Sodium	138.2mg	Fiber	0.21g

Ground Meat and Bean Casserole

1) 1/2 pound extra lean ground beef
2) 1/2 cup onion, chopped
3) 2 (16 ounce) cans baked beans
4) 1/4 cup catsup

Brown ground meat in skillet. Add onion and cook until tender. Add beans and catsup and heat thoroughly. 6 Servings.

Per Serving:

Calories	185.9	Protein	10.64g
Total Fat	8.23g	Carbohydrate	19.42g
Saturated Fat	3.24g	Cholesterol	28.41mg
Sodium	446.1mg	Fiber	4.16g

Low-fat Recipe Samples from Volume I and II:

Sherried Beef

Volume I

1) 2 pounds lean beef, cut in 1 1/2-inch cubes
2) 2 cans cream of Healthy Request mushroom soup
3) 1/2 cup cooking sherry
4) 1/2 package dry onion soup mix

Mix all ingredients in casserole and bake covered at 250 degrees for 3 hours. Good served with rice. 8 Servings.

Per Serving:

Calories	224.4	Protein	25.77g
Total Fat	7.41g	Carbohydrate	9.12g
Saturated Fat	2.06g	Cholesterol	64.73mg
Sodium	1003mg	Fiber	0.37g

Beef Roast

Volume II

1) 3 pound eye of round roast
2) Cracked peppercorns
3) Garlic to taste (optional)
4) Pepper to taste (optional)

Preheat oven to 500 degrees. Roll roast in peppercorns and season with pepper if desired. Place in baking dish, then in preheated oven. Bake 5 to 6 minutes per pound. Turn oven off and leave roast in oven for 2 more hours. DO NOT OPEN OVEN DURING THIS TIME. Bake uncovered for medium done roast. 8 Servings.

Per Serving:

Calories	224.5	Protein	37.00g
Total Fat	7.31g	Carbohydrate	0g
Saturated Fat	2.52g	Cholesterol	91.85mg
Sodium	90.15mg	Fiber	0g

Trimming all external fat from lean beef reduces the total fat content by an average of over 50 percent. When looking for the leanest cuts of beef, remember this rule of thumb: Look for the words "round" or "loin" — beef eye round, top round, round tip, top sirloin, top loin and tenderloin. If you are trying to reduce the fat content in your diet, be aware and reduce serving sizes — especially with beef and other meats.

Desserts

Orange Angel Food Cake

1) 1 package angel food cake mix
2) 3/4 cup frozen orange juice concentrate, thawed
3) 1 (8 ounce) container lite Cool Whip
4) 1/2 cup plain low-fat yogurt

Prepare angel food cake as directed on package, but pour 1/3 cup of thawed orange juice into a 2-cup measure and add enough water for the mixture to equal the amount of water called for in package directions. Bake according to directions. Cool. Combine Cool Whip, yogurt and remaining orange juice concentrate. Spoon orange sauce on individual slices of cake. 12 Servings.

Per Serving:

Calories	206.8	Protein	5.42g
Total Fat	0.93g	Carbohydrate	44.26g
Saturated Fat	0.68g	Cholesterol	0.62mg
Sodium	113.9mg	Fiber	0.14g

Chocolate Angel Cake

1) 1 package angel food cake mix
2) 1/3 cup unsweetened cocoa powder

Prepare cake mix according to package directions. Sift cocoa powder and add to cake mix. Then continue as directed on package. 12 Servings.

Per Serving:

Calories	164.6	Protein	4.97g
Total Fat	.36g	Carbohydrate	36.75g
Saturated Fat	.19g	Cholesterol	0mg
Sodium	108.6mg	Fiber	.73g

Angel Cake

1) 1 package white angel food cake mix
2) 1 cup skim milk
3) 1 (1 ounce) package milk chocolate sugar free instant pudding mix
4) 2 cups (16 ounces) lite Cool Whip

Prepare cake according to package directions for tube pan. Split cake horizontally to make 2 layers. Beat milk and pudding mix until well blended. Fold in Cool Whip. Frost layers and top of cake. Refrigerate at least 1 hour before serving. 12 Servings.

Per Serving:

Calories	202.8	Protein	5.43g
Total Fat	1.52g	Carbohydrate	41.50g
Saturated Fat	1.37g	Cholesterol	0.37mg
Sodium	151.3mg	Fiber	0g

Chocolate Glazed Angel Food Cake

1) 3 cups sifted confectioners' sugar
2) 1/4 cup unsweetened cocoa
3) 1/4 cup plus 1 1/2 tablespoons hot water
4) 1 prepared angel food cake

In bowl combine first 3 ingredients and stir until smooth. Drizzle over angel food cake. 12 Servings.

Per Serving:

Calories	287.3	Protein	4.87g
Total Fat	0.32g	Carbohydrate	68.17g
Saturated Fat	0.15g	Cholesterol	0mg
Sodium	108.8mg	Fiber	0.55g

Peach Crisp

1)   2 (16 ounce) cans sliced peaches, drained
2)   1/4 cup sugar
3)   2 teaspoons cornstarch
4)   3/4 cup low-fat Granola (without raisins)

In small bowl combine peaches, sugar and cornstarch. Spoon peach mixture into 4 custard cups coated with cooking spray. Place cups on a baking sheet and sprinkle Granola over tops of each custard cup. Bake at 400 degrees uncovered for 25 minutes or until thoroughly heated and tops are crisp. 4 Servings.

Per Serving:

Calories	167.7	Protein	2.41g
Total Fat	1.15g	Carbohydrate	39.55g
Saturated Fat	0.19g	Cholesterol	0mg
Sodium	48.64mg	Fiber	1.99g

Sugared Angel Food Cake

1)   1 1/2 cups sifted confectioners' sugar
2)   2 tablespoons skim milk
3)   1/2 teaspoon vanilla
4)   1 prepared angel food cake

In small bowl combine first three ingredients. Drizzle over angel food cake layers. 12 Servings.

Per Serving:

Calories	222.4	Protein	4.63g
Total Fat	0.08g	Carbohydrate	51.54g
Saturated Fat	0.02g	Cholesterol	0.05mg
Sodium	109.6mg	Fiber	0g

Lemon Angel Food Cake

1) 1 1/2 cups sifted confectioners' sugar
2) 2 tablespoons lemon juice, plus 1 tablespoon hot water
3) 1 teaspoon vanilla extract
4) 1 prepared angel food cake

In small bowl combine first three ingredients. Drizzle over angel food cake layers. 12 Servings.

Per Serving:

Calories	222.2	Protein	4.55g
Total Fat	0.08g	Carbohydrate	51.63g
Saturated Fat	0.01g	Cholesterol	0mg
Sodium	108.4mg	Fiber	0.01g

Shortcake Drop Biscuits

1) 1 cup self-rising flour
2) 3 tablespoons diet margarine, room temperature
3) 7 tablespoons skim milk
4) 1 teaspoon vanilla extract

Combine above ingredients until batter is blended. Drop batter by tablespoonfuls onto a nonstick cookie sheet which has been sprayed with cooking spray. Bake about 10 minutes at 450 degrees or until golden brown. This can be served with crushed berries, peaches or other fresh fruit. 8 Servings.

Per Serving:

Calories	78.30	Protein	1.99g
Total Fat	2.24g	Carbohydrate	12.15g
Saturated Fat	0.38g	Cholesterol	0.24mg
Sodium	252.5mg	Fiber	0.51g

Oatmeal Macaroons

1)   2 egg whites
2)   1/3 cup maple syrup
3)   1 cup rolled oats
4)   1/2 cup grated coconut

Beat egg whites until stiff. Combine syrup and oats in separate bowl and mix until well blended. Add coconut. Fold in beaten whites. Drop by teaspoonful (walnut size) onto lightly greased cookie sheet. Bake at 350 degrees for 15 minutes.
Makes 30 Servings.

Per Serving:
Calories	27.72	Protein	0.71g
Total Fat	0.75g	Carbohydrate	4.94g
Saturated Fat	0.51g	Cholesterol	0mg
Sodium	8.05mg	Fiber	0.34g

Chocolate Ginger Spice Squares

1)   1 package dry gingerbread mix
2)   2 (3.4 ounce) packages fat-free chocolate pudding mix
       (not instant)
3)   1/4 teaspoon ground cinnamon
4)   1 cup water

Combine above ingredients in a mixing bowl. Beat 1 minute on medium speed. Pour into 13x9x2-inch nonstick cake pan and bake at 350 degrees for 35 minutes. Allow to cool slightly or chill. Cut into squares. 32 Servings.

Per Serving:
Calories	74.15	Protein	0.88g
Total Fat	1.95g	Carbohydrate	13.84g
Saturated Fat	0.50g	Cholesterol	0mg
Sodium	154.9mg	Fiber	0.04g

Gingerale Baked Apples

1) 4 baking apples
2) 4 tablespoons golden raisins
3) 4 teaspoons brown sugar
4) 1/2 cup gingerale

Core apples without cutting through the bottom. Stand apples in baking dish just large enough to hold them. Place 1 tablespoon raisins and 1 teaspoon brown sugar in center of each apple. Pour in the gingerale. Bake at 350 degrees for 45 minutes, basting frequently, until apples are tender but not mushy. Serve warm or chilled. 4 Servings.

Per Serving:

Calories	122.8	Protein	0.55g
Total Fat	0.54g	Carbohydrate	31.88g
Saturated Fat	0.09g	Cholesterol	0mg
Sodium	2.85mg	Fiber	4.09g

Bananas Rosanna

1) 1 pint fresh strawberries
2) 1 (6 ounce) can orange juice concentrate, thawed and undiluted
3) 3 large ripe bananas, sliced
4) 1 (8 ounce) carton fat-free Cool Whip

Wash, hull and cut up strawberries. Combine them in blender with undiluted orange juice concentrate and blend until smooth. Alternate banana slices with strawberry-orange sauce. Top with Cool Whip. Serve chilled. 8 Servings.

Per Serving:

Calories	140.1	Protein	1.30g
Total Fat	0.40g	Carbohydrate	32.24g
Saturated Fat	0.09g	Cholesterol	0mg
Sodium	17.35mg	Fiber	2.10g

Pineapple Coconut Sherbet

1) 2 (8 ounce) cans unsweetened crushed pineapple in own juice, drained
2) 2 cups non-fat vanilla yogurt
3) 1/2 cup unsweetened shredded coconut
4) 2 tablespoons honey

Combine all ingredients and stir well. Pour into shallow pan and freeze until partially set. Transfer to a bowl and beat 4 minutes. Pour into a container with cover and freeze until solid. Soften at room temperature for about 15 minutes before serving.
8 Servings.

Per Serving:

Calories	116.3	Protein	2.93g
Total Fat	2.06g	Carbohydrate	22.22g
Saturated Fat	1.83g	Cholesterol	1.25mg
Sodium	54.19mg	Fiber	0.65g

Chocolate Express

1) 6 tablespoons chocolate liqueur
2) 1 envelope plain gelatin
3) 1 1/2 cups hot black coffee
4) 2 cups fat-free chocolate ice cream

Combine liqueur and gelatin in blender container. Wait for 1 minute, then add hot coffee. Cover and blend until gelatin granules are dissolved. Add ice cream and blend until smooth. Pour into 4 custard cups and chill until set. 4 Servings.

Per Serving:

Calories	215.2	Protein	4.49g
Total Fat	0.08g	Carbohydrate	36.56g
Saturated Fat	0g	Cholesterol	0mg
Sodium	77.21mg	Fiber	0g

Sherried Fruit

1)   1 (12 ounce) package mixed berries
2)   2 cups cantaloupe balls
3)   1 (8 ounce) can pineapple chunks
4)   1/4 cup cooking sherry

Combine fruit in large bowl. Add sherry and toss lightly. Cover and chill at least 2 hours or overnight. Serve chilled. 6 Servings.

Per Serving:

Calories	75.04	Protein	0.87g
Total Fat	0.33g	Carbohydrate	18.56g
Saturated Fat	0g	Cholesterol	0g
Sodium	21.96mg	Fiber	2.76g

Frozen Blueberry-Banana Dessert

1)   2 cup non-fat vanilla frozen yogurt
2)   2 bananas
3)   1 cup frozen blueberries
4)   1/4 cup frozen concentrated apple juice

Thaw frozen yogurt just enough to cut into chunks. In blender puree yogurt and remaining ingredients. Serve immediately or freeze for 15 minutes before serving. 6 Servings.

Per Serving:

Calories	141.2	Protein	3.23g
Total Fat	0.39g	Carbohydrate	32.25g
Saturated Fat	0.08g	Cholesterol	0mg
Sodium	33.64mg	Fiber	1.66g

Gingersnap-Baked Pears

1) 1 (16 ounce) can unsweetened pear halves, drained
2) 12 low-fat gingersnaps, finely crushed
3) 2 tablespoons sugar
4) 2 tablespoons low-fat margarine, melted

Arrange pears, cut side up, in a 9-inch cake pan. Combine remaining ingredients. Spread over pears. Bake at 300 degrees for 20 minutes. Serve warm. 4 Servings.

Per Serving:

Calories	151.7	Protein	0.91g
Total Fat	4.65g	Carbohydrate	26.25g
Saturated Fat	0.83g	Cholesterol	0mg
Sodium	224.2mg	Fiber	2.45g

Cappuccino Ice

1) 3 cups strong brewed coffee
2) 2 cups lite Cool Whip, thawed
3) 2 tablespoons sugar
4) 2 tablespoons cocoa

Combine all ingredients in blender. Blend at low speed until smooth. Pour into 8-inch square baking pan, cover and freeze until firm. Remove from freezer and let frozen mixture stand at room temperature for 30 minutes. Again spoon into blender and process until smooth. Return to baking pan, cover and freeze until firm. When ready to serve, let stand 5 minutes at room temperature and spoon into serving dishes. 6 Servings.

Per Serving:

Calories	64.81	Protein	0.45g
Total Fat	2.90g	Carbohydrate	8.06g
Saturated Fat	2.81g	Cholesterol	0mg
Sodium	2.74mg	Fiber	0.55g

Granola Sundae

1)   1 cup low-fat vanilla yogurt
2)   1 cup low-fat Granola mix
3)   2 cups bananas, sliced
4)   1 pint strawberries, washed and sliced

Layer yogurt, Granola and fruit into four 8-ounce stemmed glasses or bowls. Refrigerate until ready to serve. 4 Servings.

Per Serving:

Calories	280.8	Protein	6.61g
Total Fat	3.07g	Carbohydrate	62.09g
Saturated Fat	0.47g	Cholesterol	2.50mg
Sodium	91.87mg	Fiber	5.91g

Company Peach Delight

1)   2 (16 ounce) cans lite peach halves
2)   4 tablespoons fat-free cream cheese
3)   6 tablespoons brown sugar
4)   1 teaspoon ground cinnamon

Fill center of peaches with 1 tablespoon cream cheese and place halves together. Combine brown sugar and cinnamon. Roll peaches in brown sugar mixture. Chill until ready to serve. 4 Servings.

Per Serving:

Calories	133.1	Protein	2.96g
Total Fat	0.06g	Carbohydrate	32.41mg
Saturated Fat	0g	Cholesterol	0mg
Sodium	86.41mg	Fiber	1.80g

Strawberry Pineapple Cups

1) 3 ripe bananas
2) 3 (6 ounce) containers Yoplait low-fat yogurt (any flavor)
3) 1 (10 ounce) package frozen strawberries, thawed and undrained
4) 1 (8 ounce) can crushed pineapple, undrained

Line 18 medium muffin cups with paper baking cups. In medium bowl, mash bananas with fork. Stir in remaining ingredients and spoon into cups. Freeze at least 3 hours or until firm. Remove from paper cups and let stand 10 minutes before serving. 18 Servings.

Per Serving:

Calories	44.46	Protein	1.44g
Total Fat	0.11g	Carbohydrate	10.02g
Saturated Fat	0.04g	Cholesterol	0mg
Sodium	15.07mg	Fiber	0.91g

Pineapple Melba

1) 1 fresh pineapple, market sliced into 12 rings
2) 3 tablespoons sugar
3) 1 (8 ounce) can sliced peaches, drained
4) 1/2 cup raspberries

Place pineapple rings on serving plate. Sprinkle with sugar. In blender, blend peaches until smooth. Top pineapple with peach sauce and fresh raspberries. 12 Servings.

Per Serving:

Calories	40.40	Protein	0.29g
Total Fat	0.21g	Carbohydrate	10.29g
Saturated Fat	0.01g	Cholesterol	0mg
Sodium	0.97mg	Fiber	0.98g

Pumpkin Ice Cream Pie Filling

1) 1 (18 ounce) can pumpkin pie mix
2) 1 pint fat-free vanilla ice cream
3) 1/2 cup brown sugar
4) 2 tablespoons fat-free margarine

Beat pumpkin pie and ice cream together. Spoon into a prepared light graham cracker crust. Freeze 1 hour. In saucepan heat brown sugar and margarine to boiling. Remove from heat and drizzle over pie. Freeze until firm. Let pie stand at room temperature 15 minutes before serving. 8 Servings.

Pie Filling Per Serving:

Calories	151.7	Protein	2.70g
Total Fat	0.08g	Carbohydrate	36.15g
Saturated Fat	0.04g	Cholesterol	0mg
Sodium	188.7mg	Fiber	0g

Strawberry Dream Pie Filling

1) 1 (10 ounce) package frozen sweetened strawberry halves, defrosted
2) 1 (.3 ounce) package sugar-free strawberry Jello
3) 1 (8 ounce) container fat-free strawberry yogurt
4) 2 cups fat-free vanilla ice cream, softened

In mixing bowl, combine strawberry halves, Jello and yogurt. Add ice cream and mix until well combined. Pour into a prepared light graham cracker pie crust. Place in freezer for at least 4 hours before serving. Let stand at room temperature for 30 minutes before serving. Makes 8 servings of pie filling.

Pie Filling Per Serving:

Calories	212.7	Protein	4.94g
Total Fat	3.05g	Carbohydrate	41.21g
Saturated Fat	1.00g	Cholesterol	0.83mg
Sodium	171.1mg	Fiber	1.67g

Cherry Vanilla Trifle

1) 1 fat-free prepared angel food cake, torn into bite-size pieces
2) 2 (8 ounce) containers fat-free cherry vanilla yogurt
3) 4 containers prepared Jello fat-free vanilla pudding snacks
4) 1 (20 ounce) can sweet cherries, drained

Combine yogurt and pudding. Beginning with cake pieces, place a layer of cake with a layer of yogurt/pudding mix. Sprinkle with cherries. Repeat, ending with yogurt/pudding mixture. Cover and refrigerate. 10 Servings.

Per Serving:

Calories	172.3	Protein	5.02g
Total Fat	0.28g	Carbohydrate	38.13g
Saturated Fat	0.04g	Cholesterol	0mg
Sodium	346.4mg	Fiber	0.83g

Pineapple Orange Fluff

1) 1 (3 ounce) package sugar-free orange Jello
2) 1 (15 ounce) can crushed pineapple, undrained
3) 2 cups buttermilk
4) 1 (8 ounce) container fat-free Cool Whip

Heat crushed pineapple and add orange Jello. Stir until Jello is dissolved. Cool about 15 minutes. Add buttermilk and Cool Whip. Stir until blended and refrigerate until firm. 10 Servings.

Per Serving:

Calories	87.12	Protein	2.14g
Total Fat	0.43g	Carbohydrate	16.61g
Saturated Fat	0.27g	Cholesterol	1.72mg
Sodium	90.21mg	Fiber	0.38g

Brownie Cookies

1) 1 (18 ounce) package Krusteaz fat-free fudge brownie mix
2) 1/3 cup water
3) 1/3 cup confectioners' sugar
4) Pinch cinnamon (optional)

Preheat oven to 375 degrees. Mix brownie mix with water. Form into 1-inch balls. Dip into confectioners' sugar, with a pinch of cinnamon if desired, and place onto nonstick cookie sheet. Bake for 8 to 10 minutes. 32 Cookies.

Per Serving:

Calories	64.93	Protein	0.50g
Total Fat	0g	Carbohydrate	15.27g
Saturated Fat	0g	Cholesterol	0mg
Sodium	79.96mg	Fiber	0.50g

Triple Raspberry Cream

1) 1 (8 ounce) package fat-free cream cheese, room temperature
2) 1 (12 ounce) can country raspberry frozen concentrate juice, softened
3) 10 raspberry flavored fruit fat-free Newton cookies, softened
4) 1 quart fat-free no sugar raspberry ice cream

Cream cheese until fluffy. Gradually add juice concentrate and beat until well combined. Add softened ice cream and beat. Process cookies until they make a fine crumb. Place 1/2 of ice cream mixture in bottom of 8x8-inch square pan. Sprinkle with cookie crumbs (reserving 2 tablespoons for topping). Place remainder of cream mixture on top of cookie layer. Sprinkle with cookie crumbs. Freeze. 12 Servings.

Per Serving:

Calories	187.6	Protein	5.34g
Total Fat	0g	Carbohydrate	40.52g
Saturated Fat	0g	Cholesterol	0mg
Sodium	185.6mg	Fiber	0.41g

Snow Topped Brownie Mounds

1) 1 package Krusteaz fat-free brownie mix
2) 1/3 cup water
3) 45 (about 1/2 cup) miniature marshmallows
4) Pinch of cinnamon (optional)

Combine mix and water. Add a pinch of cinnamon if desired. It will be very stiff and sticky. When mix is thoroughly moistened, make small 1-inch balls. Place balls in mini-muffin pans that have been sprayed with cooking spray. Push one miniature marshmallow into each cookie ball. Bake at 350 degrees for 8 to 10 minutes. Makes 45 cookies.

Per Serving:

Calories	43.71	Protein	0.36g
Total Fat	0g	Carbohydrate	10.23g
Saturated Fat	0g	Cholesterol	0mg
Sodium	56.52mg	Fiber	0.35g

Banana Cream Pudding

1) 1 (.9 ounce) package fat-free sugar-free Jello banana cream pudding mix
2) 2 1/2 cups low-fat milk
3) 12 reduced fat vanilla wafers
4) 2 bananas, sliced

Mix pudding with milk. Layer 6 cookies, 1 sliced banana and half of pudding. Repeat layers with remaining ingredients ending with pudding. Refrigerate. 6 Servings.

Per Serving:

Calories	136.9	Protein	4.63g
Total Fat	2.93g	Carbohydrate	24.39g
Saturated Fat	1.36g	Cholesterol	7.29mg
Sodium	318.2mg	Fiber	1.16g

Low-Fat Vanilla Frosting

1) 1 (16 ounce) carton fat-free vanilla yogurt
2) 1/2 cup confectioners' sugar
3) 1/2 teaspoon vanilla

Mix above ingredients until well blended. Refrigerate until chilled. Spread on cake just before serving. Makes 2 cups.

Per Serving:

Calories	61.12	Protein	3.25g
Total Fat	0g	Carbohydrate	12.46g
Saturated Fat	0g	Cholesterol	1.25mg
Sodium	40.08mg	Fiber	0g

Orange Topping

1) 1 cup orange juice
2) 2 tablespoons cornstarch
3) 1 orange, peeled and sectioned

In saucepan, mix the cornstarch with a small amount of juice. Add remaining juice and stir over medium heat until thickened. Cool slightly. Mix orange slices with juice mixture and pour over cake. Makes topping for 8 servings.

Per Serving:

Calories	29.06	Protein	0.41g
Total Fat	0.10g	Carbohydrate	6.89g
Saturated Fat	0.01g	Cholesterol	0mg
Sodium	0.49mg	Fiber	0.47g

Meringue Shell

1) 3 egg whites, room temperature
2) 1/2 cup sugar

Preheat oven to 300 degrees. Lightly grease 9-inch pie pan. Beat egg whites until foamy. Gradually add sugar a tablespoon at a time and continue to beat until moist and stiff peaks form when beater is withdrawn. Spoon into pie pan so that it covers bottom and sides. Bake for 1 hour until light brown. Cool before filling. Good filled with fresh fruit.

Per Serving:

Calories	70.41	Protein	1.76g
Total Fat	0g	Carbohydrate	16.19g
Saturated Fat	0g	Cholesterol	0mg
Sodium	27.60	Fiber	0g

Meringue

1) 3 egg whites
2) 1/4 teaspoon cream of tartar
3) 1/2 teaspoon vanilla extract
4) 6 tablespoons sugar

Beat egg whites with cream of tartar and vanilla until soft peaks form. Gradually add sugar while beating until stiff and glossy. Spread meringue on pie filling, sealing against edge. Bake for 15 minutes or until peaks are golden brown.

Per Serving:

Calories	54.90	Protein	1.76g
Total Fat	0g	Carbohydrate	12.18g
Saturated Fat	0g	Cholesterol	0mg
Sodium	27.56mg	Fiber	0g

Low Fat & Light Four Ingredient Cookbook

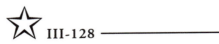

Index

B

BEEF,